FINDING JOY

FINDING JOY

JOY

101 Ways to Free Your Spirit and Dance with Life

CHARLOTTE DAVIS KASL, PH.D.

Illustrations by Lenore Davis

HarperPerennial

A Division of HarperCollinsPublishers

A hardcover edition of this book was published in 1994 by HarperCollins Publishers.

FINDING JOY: 101 WAYS TO FREE YOUR SPIRIT AND DANCE WITH LIFE. Copyright © 1994 by Charlotte Davis Kasl. Illustrations copyright © 1994 by Lenore Davis. All rights reserved. Printed in the United States of America. No part of this book may be used or reproduced in any manner whatsoever without written permission except in the case of brief quotations embodied in critical articles and reviews. For information address Harper-Collins Publishers, Inc., 10 East 53rd Street, New York, NY 10022.

HarperCollins books may be purchased for educational, business, or sales promotional use. For information please write: Special Markets Department, HarperCollins Publishers, Inc., 10 East 53rd Street, New York, NY 10022.

First HarperPerennial edition published 1994.

Designed by Janet Tingey

The Library of Congress has catalogued the hardcover edition as follows:

Kasl, Charlotte Davis.
  Finding joy : 101 ways to free your spirit and dance with life / Charlotte Davis Kasl ; illustrations by Lenore Davis. — 1st ed.
    p. cm.
  ISBN 0-06-017071-9
  1. Spiritual life. 2. Joy. 3. Conduct of life. I. Title.
BL624.K3375   1994
158'. 1—dc20   93-21283

ISBN 0-06-092588-4 (pbk.)
94 95 96 97 98 ❖/HC 10 9 8 7 6 5 4 3 2 1

To a bountiful supply of love and compassion on the planet so that all people may be fed, have shelter, be safe, and experience joy.

also to
Margaret Wickes MacDonald and Gail Derrick

CONTENTS

TAPPING THE POWER OF YOUR MIND
A Training Manual for the Brain

LIGHTEN UP
Finding Balance in a Crazy World

MARVEL AT YOUR AMAZING BODY

REACHING OUT, BREAKING THE RULES
Tips for Making Life Easier

WHEN YOU'RE SINKING, GRAB A LIFE LINE

LOVING YOUR BODY
IN SPITE OF IT ALL

LOVING CHILDREN,
DISCOVERING OURSELVES

MORE YEARS, MORE WISDOM

DANCING WITH LIFE

JOY TO THE WORLD

ACKNOWLEDGMENTS

My heartfelt thanks to: Janet Goldstein, my editor, for faith, humor, and guidance in shaping this book; Edite Kroll, my agent, who provided wonderful support and friendship every step of the way; Lenore Davis, my sister, who worked very hard to create images for this book; and Lois Greenlee, who took over my office, bringing dedication, humor, and remarkable skill to the job.

I send gratitude to Ken Keyes and the whole community at Cornucopia (in 1980) whose teachings and training made a profound difference in my life. Your wisdom echoes through these pages. To Kay Detweiler, whose support and enthusiasm sing in my heart whenever I feel alone, blessings and joy always. And to the late Margaret Wickes MacDonald whose magnificent spirit, love, and humor blessed my life, you live in my heart.

Joy and best wishes to the people who welcomed me so warmly to my new home and new Quaker meeting in Montana: Beverly Young and Tom Javins, Lindsay Richards and Tom Roberts, Grace and Bob Lucas, Lavern and Franklin Kohl. I also thank the Kester and Smith families, who bring special meaning to the word *neighbor.* And to my special circle of spiritual travelers, Reggie Windham, Jeanette Stangl, and Barbara Spring, bright blessings, wild adventures, and happy howling in the moonlight. I am so glad to know you.

I also send warm wishes and appreciation to all the people who have written letters responding to my books. Your letters are like sparklers of energy, encouraging me and supporting me in my work. Finally, to all the courageous people I have journeyed with in therapy, you have taught me well, brought me joy, and repeatedly deepened my faith in the capacity of the human spirit to heal and grow. To all of you I send courage, peace, love, and joy.

AN INVITATION TO FINDING JOY

JOY IS GOOD FOR YOU

Joy has the power to open our hearts, remove fear, instill hope, and foster healing. Joy leads us to wisdom because it connects us to all we are—our mind, heart, power, and spirit. Joy stimulates our immune system, increases our energy, and gives us mental clarity. It helps us heighten our level of consciousness so we can more readily tap our inner wisdom. Instead of agonizing over decisions, we become more able to simply listen within and Know what to do.

As we open ourselves to joy we experience the breadth of human emotions, realize our connection to all life, feel compassion, and dance lightly with the dramas of our lives. As our joy expands we feel deeply connected to ourselves and to something bigger than ourselves.

When we have the ability to access joy, we are more able to stay centered in the midst of life's difficulties and tap our creativity. This helps our creativity pour forth uncensored by our rational minds. We become able to recapture the spontaneity of childhood before we were taught to stop our wild scribbling and start coloring within the lines. Creativity that springs from joy also helps us reach beyond the boundaries of traditional thought for new, original, compassionate solutions to the problems and challenges of our lives and our society.

Joy is not about getting "high," or prolonged indulgence in sense pleasures. While enjoying our senses in a balanced way helps us touch the experience of joy, ultimately joy comes from moving beyond our senses to a deeper experience of stillness and inner Knowing. Once we touch this place, even momentarily, our lives are altered because we become aware of the vast resources of our intricately interwoven body, mind, and spirit in shaping the course of our lives. When we develop our capacity for joy, it lives within us like a wellspring of awareness that heightens our ability to be intimate with others without fear.

JOY IS YOUR NATURAL BIRTHRIGHT

We are all born with a capacity for love and joy. Yet many of us feel uneasy at the thought of seeking more joy in our lives. That is not surprising because we have been taught repeatedly that growth comes through struggle and suffering. Joy and happiness are suspect in our culture, often regarded as childlike, indulgent, or immature. Our culture is focused on competition, control, activity, striving, and productivity.

While you may not have been taught directly that quietness or idleness are to be feared, it is an undercurrent that pervades our culture. An echo of the old phrase—"Idle brains are the devil's workshop"—still lingers in many people's minds, creating uneasiness, guilt, or discomfort at the idea of relaxing or doing things solely for pleasure and delight. Yet the journey to joy includes allowing ourselves time to do nothing, be idle and let our inner world be known. An idle mind helps us to slip beneath the activities of our daily lives into the quiet Knowing place that resides in each of us, a place at once secure, peaceful, and vast.

Our culture may fear joy, because joy empowers people to feel alive, exuberant, self-respecting, and unlikely to tolerate being exploited or harmed. Thus becoming a joyful happy person can feel like a crime against the powers that be, an act of arrogance or willfulness that is somehow wrong. But it is not wrong. An inner sense of joy is our spirit coming alive.

Our culture also emphasizes control and obedience which is based on fear—fear that people allowed free expression of emotions and thoughts will go out of control, rebel, be lazy or deceitful. Thus people become divided inside, their passion, anger, and tears constricted like an unseen enemy that could attack if not closely guarded. People fear they will cry forever if they let themselves feel sad, become violent if they allow themselves to vent their rage, or gain one hundred pounds if they allow themselves pleasure with food. For many, constant external striving and control of our natural joys lead to a point where our inner child or spirit rebels, yelling, "Enough of all this work, let's go outside and play."

When we don't listen to this healthy rebellion we are likely to experience anxiety, depression, or lack of energy. When we deny ourselves natural joys we tend to substitute counterfeit joys— substances, sex, food, status, activity, new cars, new hairdos, fewer wrinkles, and snazzy clothes. It's the right search at the wrong door because true joy is not something we buy off a shelf, but rather it is a richness of spirit that dwells within and is expressed through our relationships to others.

I believe we are born blessed as an integral part of all creation. We all have the potential to access our inner world that leads to joy and peace. Sometimes we encounter this quiet resting place much easier than we expect. Other times it is illusive, something just outside our grasp. But it is always there.

JOY IS GOOD FOR THE PLANET

A truly joyful person transmits healing energy to all around them. And when we collectively start to feel joy, our ability to love each other expands enormously. From this place we can move toward resolving differences between groups of people and hopefully evolve to a level where we feel compassion and care for all life on this planet. Joy is also good for the earth because we take care of the things we love. If we love the earth and feel nourished by its beauty and recognize that it sustains us, then we will want to preserve it.

Joy helps us release our judgments and be with people in a rich, flowing way that sparks our energy and leaves us fulfilled and satisfied. It removes the jealousy and restlessness that lead to greed and exploitation and helps us create a circle of kindness and healing. When people experience more happiness and contentment, they want fewer things and have more desire to be of service. When people can be of service and feel purpose in their lives they connect with their spirit and with joy.

This book invites you to imagine a world where joy and love, rather than unhappiness, depression, and suffering are seen as the natural order of things. We need joy because greed, scarcity, fear, alienation, and addiction, which come from a lack of joy, have not been good for our lives or our planet. We need joy to help us all become part of an expanding web of wisdom, compassion, and love.

THE JOURNEY OF FINDING JOY

I decided to write about joy because I want to feel more joy. I have traveled a long journey away from the depression and hopelessness that permeated my late teens and twenties. I have found that a sense of inner joy has become the mooring that grounds my life and gives me a safe home I can always return to. I am fascinated with the dance of slipping in and out of joy, and finding ways to bring back the experience. I also write with the hope that these steps, which have been central to my journey, can be of help to others. They have been helpful to many of the people who came to me as clients over the past sixteen years. It has been like a circle of creativity and information we have woven together. I teach what I am learning, and clients take the information, experiment with it, expand it, and bring me a new perspective.

Just as overcoming depression and moving toward joy in my life has been like putting the pieces of a mosaic together to create a whole, this book on joy is a mosaic of steps that can be used in any order. So welcome and best wishes.

Charlotte Kasl
Lolo, Montana
October, 1993

DISCOVERING THE
POWER OF JOY

1. AWAKEN YOUR INNER FIRE

Joy is a source of personal power. Joy awakens as we open ourselves to the wonder of the universe both inside us and around us. As we allow the expansive power of joy to flow through us, our awareness expands and we see beyond the concrete world to a world of love, intimacy, creativity, and wisdom.

We create room for joy as we move beyond "shoulds" and "musts" to an expansive state where we accept our capacity to be both powerful and gentle, expansive and reclusive, delighted and bored, wise and confused, passive and assertive, giving and receptive, generous and withholding, frightened and adventuresome, angry and loving. As we become accepting of ourselves we are more able to reach inside and speak our truths: Yes, No, I want, I can, I feel, I believe, I see, I love. This is a form of self-love that creates unity and peacefulness within because we are living at one with our wisest self.

Joy leads us to the heart of our spiritual journey because it ignites the fire of transformation that enables us to change our thoughts, perceptions, and feelings. In doing so we are able to transcend an empty, humdrum existence and infuse our lives with vitality, awareness, and the ability to move beyond the limited boundaries of self. Finding joy doesn't mean life will always be easy, rather life becomes rich because we live near the pulse of possibility. To open the door you can start by saying, I am willing. I am willing to feel, to Know, to love, and to expand. I am willing to let the concrete walls of my beliefs slip away and move into a new level of awareness.

In his "Ode to Joy," the German poet Friedrich Schiller wrote, "By that holy fire impassioned, to thy sanctuary we come." When we allow ourselves to feel joy, we create an inner sanctuary, a home for the soul that allows us to feel safe to laugh, cry, be angry, question, and think for ourselves. When we create this home for truth and delight, we feel a sense of inner strength. Unkind remarks and difficult situations lose their ability to singe our souls or tear at our hearts because we are no longer candles in the wind. Rather, we become the fire of life itself—a being, an identity that cannot be blown about or extinguished by external events because we accept all of who we are.

2. REMEMBER JOY AND FIND HOPE

Hope is the thing with feathers
That perches in the soul
And sings the tune without the words
And never stops, at all.

Emily Dickinson

Joy brings hope and hope brings joy. Imagine joy as a memory dwelling within you—a bird perched on your soul singing a song of hope. Let yourself know it is always there. Sometimes we lose contact with that voice and feel despair. In those times, if we can remember that the *potential* for joy lives within us, we may regain hope and find the strength to take steps to improve our lives.

If you feel down, blue, depressed, or tend to be hard on yourself, take time to remember the good things you have done for yourself, the risks you have taken, the ways you have survived. Remember times when you experienced contentment or joy. Then hold these images in your heart and tell yourself you can re-create them. You have the power to create happiness in your life—the potential for joy is within you. You might ask yourself what in your life right now blocks you from feeling joy, and consider what you need to do to get on a path toward greater happiness.

The bird of joy that "perches in the soul" never stops singing—we just stop listening. When we can hear the promise of joy within us, we have more power to come alive to our desire for life.

3. PREPARE FOR JOY

Joy may seem illusive or fleeting, yet there is a path we can walk that brings the delight, passion, and sweetness of joy into our lives, sweeping over us, filling us, transporting us, making life feel worth the trouble. Joy may appear to come suddenly, but in reality we prepare for joy every time we speak our truths, care for ourselves, expand our knowledge, nurture our friendships, let people love us, take on new adventures, and go where our hearts lead us.

My friend Janet is about to have her second baby. She has developed a strong bond with her husband; created a cozy living space, a network of friends, a good job; has read a great deal on parenting; and has enjoyed her first child. She has also spent many years investing in her personal growth. In other words, over the years she has built a nest for herself, both physical and emotional, that enables joy to flourish amid the fears and difficulties of having a new child.

Preparation for joy can span the decades of our lives and even go back to the time of our ancestors. For example, I am currently making plans to go backpacking. Preparation began a couple of months ago when I started working out at a gym to strengthen my leg muscles. Or perhaps preparation started even earlier, when I took a racketball class fifteen years ago in an attempt to get regular exercise. Or was it when I was a child, and experienced the wonder and joy of hiking with my father in the pristine forests and mountains of Montana? Is that when I started preparing? I remember back even further, to stories from my grandmother, a botanist, about taking her young children out in the woods for walks and picnics, and I realize that joy is passed down through the ages. It is a paradox to say we are always preparing for joy, because when we prepare for joy—living by love and our heart's desire—we are experiencing it as well.

4. LET JOY INTO YOUR BEING

Genuine poetry can communicate before it is understood.
T.S. Eliot

Joy is like *genuine poetry*. It communicates to us in the whole of our being and seems beyond words. Have you ever had a wonderful experience and felt it go clunk inside when you tried to explain it to someone? That's because the words could not capture the essence of the experience and the listener could not connect it to his or her own experience.

Recently, I revisited my college poetry books, which sat untouched for thirty years. As I took them down I remembered how I had felt lost, irritated, and uneasy in a college course because I couldn't understand the literal meaning of much of the poetry. Others would discuss this word or that, pondering its *true* meaning or symbolism. I would be amazed and fascinated, but something was missing. It was like looking at a dissected

frog, seeing all the parts, but losing the essence of the frog. I never said a word in class for fear of being thought stupid, and I wondered how I'd pass the course.

Yet I loved to read the lyric poems of Emily Dickinson and the sonnets of Shakespeare because of their rhythm and the sweet feeling they kindled within me. Then, one day we had a Shakespeare sonnet to discuss. For the first time, as if some force propelled me, I raised my hand and said what I truly felt: "I'm reluctant to take it apart because it has such a feeling of beauty and lightness that fills me up when I read it. It's as if the whole thing creates an entity beyond words, an experience—like a piece of music." To my absolute amazement, the professor said, "That's just the right response." The class was still, and I remain forever grateful to that professor for validating my experience and keeping me from reselling my poetry books at the end of the semester.

So don't worry if you don't understand the poem of joy. Just let the feelings, the sounds, and the rhythm wash over you. You Know.

5. REMEMBER YOUR CONNECTION TO ALL

Joy comes from knowing that we are not isolated beings, rather we are all intrinsic parts of the whole human family. Knowing this kindles the awareness that, while we may feel lonely sometimes, at a deeper level we are never alone. Many Native American rituals begin or end with the words "All our Relations," to signify our connection to all who went before us, all who will come after us, and all who are now living. This brings to us a sense of the vastness of existence and reminds us of our place in the cosmic scheme of life.

We may not always remember that we are related to *all* people and *all* life throughout times past and times to come. We may not always feel it, but like fresh air waiting for us to take a deep breath, there exists within us the knowledge that we are intertwined with all living things, part of a web that extends far beyond our being or comprehension. So imagine yourself as part of this web, absolutely essential and vital to its existence. Let yourself know that you matter just as every thread in a scarf matters. When we break a thread in a woven scarf, it affects the appearance and strength of the whole scarf.

6. SEE WITH ALL YOUR SENSES

While with an eye made quiet by the power
Of harmony, and the deep power of joy
We see into the life of things.

Wordsworth

Joy brings a *heightened* state of awareness and a quiet receptivity that allow us to "see into the life of things." And conversely, when you take time to look into the life of things, you will start to feel more joy. When your senses are alive and you are in a receptive state, you can feel wonder by looking at a leaf and marveling at its lines, colors, and textures; you touch the power of creation as you image the leaf growing by absorbing water, sunlight, air, and the energy of the earth. You experience the nature of evolution in a single moment when you see a child's face light up as she takes her first step, stacks blocks, or proudly carries a package into the house feeling a sense of both mastery and belonging. When you let yourself feel pleasure by touching velvet, stroking hair, or smelling bread baking, you are tuning into the wonder of your senses and the miracle of creation.

Think back on times when you had an intensified state of awareness. Maybe you were in love, at a birth, witnessing the death of a loved one, or spending time with nature. When people are in love, the songs of birds seem magical, people look beautiful, a breeze across the face sends a sensuous ripple through the body. When a woman is giving birth, in the midst of her pain she feels the awe of creation or a connection with all women throughout time. When sitting beside a loved one as they die, an inner world of understanding and compassion wells up inside. When hiking in the mountains in a field of wildflowers, you feel a connection to your soul.

Bring this heightened state of awareness to your daily life by noticing your surroundings and thinking of their history. For example, imagine the history of a wooden table. Think back to when it was a tree in the woods. Look at the grain and see the lines, each signifying a year, and think of that tree standing all that time in one place. Then imagine it being cut down, taken to a mill, made into lumber, shipped to a furniture factory, sawed, glued, and finished. Imagine the table on a transport truck, and then in a store, and think of the people walking by and touching it. Then remember when it came into your life. It has a history, the same as we do.

A heightened state of awareness comes when we look, and then look again, and then relax into whatever situation we are in. When we have a capacity for fascination with simple things, we are able to sit peacefully for hours on a park bench, or in an airport, engrossed by the different gaits and gestures of people as they walk, talk, and stand. We develop the ability to be patient as we stand in line at the grocery store because we have the ability to look with fascination and wonder at all that surrounds us.

7. RECOGNIZE COUNTERFEIT JOYS

When we do not have a capacity to be fascinated and interested in simple things in life, we become restless and bored and go in search of quick fixes—usually some outside stimulus that entertains us or gives us a quick high. These fixes can be anything from hot fudge sundaes and caffeine to computer games, shopping sprees, loud music, a great romance, or sex. We buy, we spend, we work, we watch TV, smoke cigarettes, but we live excluded from the center of our spirit. We become derailed by the trickster of immediate gratification—the desire for a quick high, rather than a slow blooming joy that comes out of the gradual awakening of our senses, out of love, and out of a capacity for awe and wonder.

If something is a counterfeit joy, we may fear losing it or feel deprived when we can't have it. It's not so much the object we reach for, it's our emotional state. At one moment, having a cookie could be part of the path toward joy, a conscious act of celebration; at another time, it could detract from joy because we eat the cookie to repress our anger or our hurt. One question to ask is whether we do something out of fear or out of love.

Emily Dickinson wrote

Inebriate of air—am I,
And debauchee of Dew
Reeling through endless summer days
From inns of Molten Blue.

She was talking about the ability to get high just breathing air, being carefree or seeing the dew on the grass. As we journey toward joy, we dance between filling ourselves with natural highs and gently detaching from the counterfeit highs that extract a price—a hangover, shame, emptiness, or frustration. Yet we honor the needs that led us to the counterfeit joys because love, comfort, or release from pain were the positive desires that led us to consume cookies or buy fancy cars or abuse drugs.

As you detach from counterfeit joys, you may feel a pang of fear: "But I need this. I'll be lonely without it." To calm yourself, take a breath, and ask your adult self, What would happen *if:* I *didn't* open the fridge door and eat something? . . . I *didn't* rush off to town and buy something to alleviate my boredom? . . . I *didn't* turn on the TV? . . . I *didn't* go in search of sex? What would happen if I just sit here in my restlessness and feel whatever comes up? You might feel sad, angry, or lonely or go through physical withdrawal symptoms. But you will also be creating a shift in consciousness that will lead you to feel comfort with your inner world, the place where joy resides.

8. ALLOW TIME FOR PLEASURE

Imagine taking a day to be guided solely by pure delight. I once went to a workshop where the teacher talked about nurturing simplicity by feeding ourselves with joy. He would set aside a day for pleasure with no advance plans, waking up in the morning and letting images of possibilities go through his mind until one triggered delight. His days for joy took many forms—he might drive to a nearby town, read the paper at a bakery while eating wonderful bread, take a walk, go to the library, drop in on a friend, go to the country, write letters, take a few children to a museum.

For many people, allowing pleasure induces guilt because they have been taught to *be productive* and *get things accomplished.* But it's really a matter of definition. Gentle pleasures *are* productive. They're good for your health. They help you relax, put you in touch with your spirit, open your senses, and deepen your connection with your inner wisdom.

When we develop a capacity for knowing what will bring us pleasure, we can care for ourselves when we are lonely or when life is difficult. I remember one Christmas vacation when I didn't have much to do (and everyone else was burdened by too many parties). I asked myself what I could do to feel content without forcing something to happen. The idea came to me to make a lined wool bathrobe from material I had been saving for many

years. So I settled down with my sewing machine, turned on a radio, and welcomed my cats to lounge nearby. As I became absorbed in the cloth, the stitches, and the beautiful bathrobe taking shape, my loneliness was assuaged. Now, whenever I wear that bathrobe, I remember sitting in my sewing nook, the cats playing with threads and scraps of material, and feeling peaceful because I was taking care of myself when life hadn't handed me what I wanted.

9. TRUST THE WISDOM OF JOY

Joy is wisdom, time an endless song.

William Butler Yeats

Joy *is* wisdom. And wisdom is the intelligence of all our being coming alive. Thus seeing, feeling, knowing, perceiving, dreaming, and dancing lead us to to both wisdom and joy. It's like having all parts of us awake, alive, and integrated. This helps us make wise decisions. If we try to make a decision with only our head, heart, or hormones, we are missing important data. Wise decisions come when we have a committee meeting of our heart, mind, intuition, and power.

A person who is full of joy *is* wise. A person can get all A's and be a brilliant student yet have neither wisdom nor joy. This was a great source of confusion to me in my college days, when I was undiagnosed as dyslexic. I thought a part of me was stupid because I couldn't finish tests that involved reading and multiple-choice questions. So I grew up thinking that getting all A's and discussing lofty ideas would bring joy.

Later, after getting to know some "brilliant" students and engaging in intellectual conversations, I realized something was still missing. Debate and discussion can be stimulating and interesting, but joy cannot dance freely within the confines of our rational mind. So one summer day, I left my intellectual circle and headed out to a nearby lake with some old high school friends. I nestled down in the warm sand, ate grapes, chatted about nothing much, played cards, swam, and felt a sensuousness stirring in my body which gave way to a deep sense of peace and wholeness, as if I were reaching parts of me that had been asleep.

For a while I thought I had to make a decision between being an intellectual or a person sitting mindlessly on a beach. Then it occurred to me that both experiences fed me in a special way, and I didn't have to make a choice, rather to find balance between the two.

Wisdom is not about isolated facts and knowledge. The definition of a sage is a person who uses knowledge in a compassionate, intelligent way. So remember, there are no grades in the school of wisdom, just a gradual awakening of the sage within you, as you open yourself to joy and become aware of all you are.

10. ALLOW GRIEF AND OTHER SCARY FEELINGS

One of the barriers to joy is a pent-up grief, sorrow, or anger. Other barriers are the secrets we keep because we are ashamed. Burying emotions and keeping secrets is like wrapping a shield around your soul that shuts out the smells of spring, the delicacy of touch, the softness of love.

It's difficult to feel free and open when we're congested with buried pain or rage or secrets. Joy flourishes when we accept all of who we are. This includes experiencing our feelings and clearing out guilt and shame by being honest. How can we ever know we are loved if we show only a little part of ourselves to others?

I have had difficulty in my life being able to cry. Three teachings that have helped me are from the Bible: "Weeping endureth for the night, but joy cometh in the morning" and "Blessed are they that mourn, for they shall be comforted." "They that sow in tears shall reap in joy." One of the most magical aspects of human existence is that grieving, or weeping for a loss, eases pain and opens the way to reconnect with joy. Crying releases tension in the body and can lead us to reach out for comfort, which in turn bonds us to others—an important part of the path toward joy. In my work as a psychologist I frequently see people emotionally constricted by repressed grief and anger. Over the years they become divided, detached or distant or turn to addictive substances or relationships. Because the human psyche is a holistic system, to numb one part of our being is to numb the rest and create constant inner struggle. I have worked with many couples who believe the love between them is gone. Often, after they open up and express their anger, hurt, and frustrations, the love starts to return. It feels like magic, but it's not magic; it's the power of our ability to shift to new states of consciousness as we unblock the illusions that come between us and our love.

I remember saying to myself at the age of five, "I'll never let them see me cry again," because I had been teased unmercifully for crying or showing my feelings. My jaw became tight, my body felt heavy, and I endured many losses over the following years without feeling my grief or anger. Thirty years later, when the tears came back with the help of psychotherapy, I couldn't believe the torrent of sorrows I held within me. I wept for my childhood loneliness, the teacher who shamed me in the second grade, the death of my grandmother, my first solo piano recital when my mother wouldn't make a dress for me, the birthday my parents ignored, my miscarriage, the man

I left because I was afraid. Although it was painful reliving those old experiences with the feelings attached, in doing so I released huge, dense blocks of my energy, freeing me both physically and emotionally.

Crying can ease the intensity of physical pain and help us heal because by releasing tension we free the flow of our natural healing energy. Shortly after having breast cancer surgery and the lymph nodes removed from under my arm, my Native American friend Denise took me to a sweat lodge. My side was still swollen from the lymph fluid. Once we were in the sweat lodge, it was as if an unseen power helped me completely let go and weep for my pain, my fear, and my loss. Not only did my grief lose its grip on my life, the swelling under my arm receded dramatically, which is typical of how the body and mind work together.

So when we sob with grief over a loss, cry because we're hurt, respectfully express our anger and frustrations, or tell our shameful secrets, we are freeing ourselves emotionally and physically, which makes room for joy. This is a process that takes time. We need to be gentle yet remind ourselves that freedom comes when we stop repressing our feelings and honor the truths of our inner world.

11. HOLD ON TIGHTLY, LET GO LIGHTLY

He who binds to himself a joy
Does the winged life destroy
But he who kisses the joy as it flies
Lives in eternity's sunrise.

William Blake

You can open yourself to joy, but you cannot grab joy, hold onto it, or force it to come. Like a beautiful day, we can relish it, enjoy it, breathe in the fragrance, and then let it pass. Everything is continually changing, so if we demand that joy be our constant companion, we end up with disappointment. Finding joy is something of a paradox, well understood in Buddhist teachings. While Buddhism teaches a path of enlightenment, it also teaches people not to attach themselves to becoming enlightened because the striving makes you tense and separates you from the present. Joy comes from being relaxed and aware of the present moment. The goal is not to feel joy every moment, the goal is to simply be—aware, open, loving—and accept yourself when you are not.

People attach in many ways. We can attach to things ("I've just got to have that car") or people ("My life is nothing without her"), or we can have fixed expectations for holidays, dates, or family gatherings, as if we write a script for what everyone should say. This is a particularly common form of attachment. For example, a young man asks out a beautiful woman and imagines a romantic evening at a classy restaurant followed by a sexual encounter. When the woman appears in jeans and a casual shirt, says she'd like to go Dutch to Annie's Parlour, expresses excitement about a backpacking trip planned for the following day, and says she wants to be home by 10:00 P.M., the man is devastated. He had attached himself to an imaginary joy and written a script for the evening, which kept him from finding the joy of the moment.

When people lack capacity for joy—to connect, feel, and let go—they may try to capture a moment and imprison it. I remember a guided tour I once took on a boat through the canals in Amsterdam. Fortunately, I had forgotten to take my camera. As the boat took us down the canals, the guide would point out a landmark, and then, like a chorus line, all the people on the boat would turn toward the building, raise their cameras, aim, and shoot. While I understood the desire to have a souvenir to reawaken memories, I wondered how everyone else really felt at the end of the day. What was it like to see Amsterdam through a lens? Did they ever feel the breeze, take in the atmosphere of the sidewalk cafes, or absorb the essence of the place? Did they feel joy? Or did they, like a person I once knew, capture the moment in pictures to make a pretty album to show friends? Did the photo album hold more reality than the actual experience of being there?

When you look at the world through a lens, when you try to bind yourself to an experience, you lose a part of the experience. What would happen if you put away the camera, the journal, the futurizing—and simply looked, felt, and savored an experience, trusting that it was being recorded in your mind, your heart, and your spirit?

LOVING YOURSELF,
NO MATTER WHAT

12. YOU ARE PERFECTLY IMPERFECT RIGHT THIS MINUTE

You always have been perfectly imperfect, you always will be. You will make mistakes on occasion, do things you wish you hadn't done, long for things you don't have. You are capable of honesty and sneakiness, kindness and hatred, compassion and cruelty. At the same time, though, you are a perfect living being. You've been entrusted with a life that's yours to care for, enjoy, and learn from. They have no one just like you. There never will be.

Many people have an unrealistic notion of what it means to be human. People talk about "having it all together," which is an illusory notion because we are always in a state of change. They think a day will come when they no longer misplace their keys, lose their temper, offend other people, get scared, or feel at a loss for words. They might also think they should be able to stick to a diet, have a stimulating job that pays well, be liked by everyone, and wake up every day feeling bright and alert. If you really think these things are possible, look around you. Does anyone fit this description?

If you want to be happy, kiss these thoughts good-bye and send them to the winds. When they come into your mind, smile at them and watch them dance without taking them seriously. We all get lonely sometimes, spill the milk, put our foot in our mouth, get scared, or space out at an important meeting. Recognize the voices in your head for what they are: the great goblins of our parents, churches, and schools, an authoritarian approach to child rearing, the plentiful "shoulds" that gobble up self-esteem.

Remember, just because these thoughts are in your head doesn't make them true. *Perfection is in truth, honesty, and kindness as we walk our path.* The goal is not to avoid slipping off the path, it's to slide off with grace, enjoy the ride, and be kind to yourself.

13. LOOK FOR THE POSITIVE INTENTION

No matter how strange, crazy, or cruel a behavior appears to be, under every act lies a positive intention, usually a desire to feel love, power, safety, or a sense of belonging. Finding the positive intention underneath an unwanted behavior helps us understand ourselves and feel compassion rather than shame. It also helps us stop struggling inside because we bring the light of awareness to whatever is going on within us. We literally lighten up the situation.

I have found this approach to be helpful to many people, particularly to those who are depressed or berate themselves unmercifully. For example, do you often have difficulty getting out of bed in the morning? Rhona, a client who had suffered from years of depression, had this problem. She would lie in bed scolding herself, "I should get up, I know better. What's wrong with me? I'm so lazy," and on and on.

Instead of working on a behavior plan to get her out of bed, which would have been controlling the behavior but not allowing her to heal, I asked her to explore her positive intention of staying in bed. "What is nice about being in bed?" I asked her.

I saw an instant relaxation in her body as she paused to think for a moment. "It feels safe . . . cozy, and warm. No one can hurt me there."

I asked her what other places had felt safe to her, particularly as a child. Her face was instantly sad. "Nowhere," she answered. "I could never predict how my parents would be, but it was usually painful to be around them."

"So staying in bed is a way you love and protect yourself," I said.

She was quiet. "But shouldn't I try to change it?"

"Try reminding yourself of all the ways you are good to yourself by staying in bed and see what happens," I answered.

I suggested to Rhona that the next time she stayed in bed, she start sentences with "I understand . . . " or "My positive intention is . . . " The next week she reported thinking things like: "My positive intention for staying in bed is to be safe, to feel comfort. It's soft, it's warm. I'm happy here." Then, a week later, she had a realization that helped release her from guilt and shame: "I was sitting in bed and the thought popped into my mind 'I'm not a bad person for staying in bed. I'm being nice to myself' and it felt really true."

Although negative thoughts continued to dance in her mind, by focusing on the positive intention underlying her behavior, Rhona slowly gained more energy and started to feel hope. A few weeks later she spoke with a feeling of conviction. "I realized for the first time that I'm not a crazy, sick person. I got depressed from being abused and it was the only way to get attention." This was a pivotal moment in her life. She started to feel anger along with hope. After that she set limits with her parents, who called daily, and had more energy to start exercising and improving her diet.

A week later she said, "This morning while I was lying in bed saying it was safe and okay to be there, I had the thought, 'I can be safe sitting at my kitchen table.' So I got up . . . just like that."

Much of our problematic adult behavior stems from ways we protected ourselves as children. For example, the positive intention underlying using drugs or having numerous sexual partners as an adolescent could be to anesthetize the pain from incest, abuse, neglect, or poverty. The positive intention underlying suddenly clamming up when someone gets angry could be to avoid getting hit. The positive intention underlying eating lots of sugar could be to ease pangs of loneliness, or shift the focus from feeling unloved to having a stomachache.

Finding the positive intention is not an instant cure, rather it begins a process of experiencing self-acceptance. We replace our intense identification with our behavior with awareness and compassion. In essence, we are trusting that love is always present, and in this trust we find an avenue to healing and transformation.

14. BLESS TODAY:
IT WILL NEVER COME AGAIN

It's fine to work toward future goals, but don't forget that today will never come again. You have only twenty-four hours to enjoy it.

Some people put life on hold while striving for their dreams. At first their theme song is, "After I attain_____, then I'll be happy." Then, later, after the success of attaining pales, the regrets are felt. "Why didn't I take time to plant a garden?" (or play with my children, visit old friends, be kinder to my partner, relax, go to the movies, go hiking?).

Instead of waiting to be an old lady to wear purple, wear it now. Instead of waiting for retirement to live in a beautiful place, consider finding a way to get there now. When we live our lives in accordance with our dreams, it becomes easy to cheer for other people doing so. When we don't, it's easy to be sour grapes, unsupportive, or jealous when others break free and follow their heart's desire.

Recently I received a letter from my former Minneapolis neighbors. "We've put our house up for sale," it read. "We came home from the country and said, 'No more!' We don't want to live in the city so we're going to leave. We're looking at a small town in Colorado with sunny days, mild winters, and we're talking it over with our teenage children." The energy and joy jumped off the page. I could share their happiness because I knew how much I enjoyed my move to the mountains. I sent back a postcard that said, "Great! Wow! You did it and I'm glad." There was a time in my life when, because I wasn't living where I wanted to be, I would have felt a tinge of jealousy and could not have been so happy for them.

So if you feel as if your life is somewhere out there as opposed to right here, stop and ask yourself, really ask yourself:

- What is missing in my life?
- What have I put on hold?
- What am I waiting for?
- What would really fill my heart and make me happy?
- What would I regret if I died tomorrow?

Though you may not die tomorrow, the saddest death is walking around like a robot, cut off from the magic of today—from love, from beauty, from being where you want to be.

And remember, if all life is sacred, then today is sacred. Ask yourself, What am I doing to feel joy *today*? A wonderful way to start the day is to bless it:

Blessings on this day, may I make it special in some way.
Blessings on my life, may I treat it with love and care.
Blessings on all people, may I see the goodness in everyone.
Blessings on nature, may I notice its beauty and wonder.
Blessings on the truth, may it be my constant companion.

15. OBSERVE YOUR DANCE: "HMM, THAT'S INTERESTING"

An important step to self-acceptance and joy is to realize that we're all playing out a drama. It's like a dance: we waltz happily with life one day and are wallflowers the next. We get up, we fall down; we feel loved, we feel lonely. The idea is to learn from our dramas, not drown in them.

A major key to self-acceptance is to *observe* ourselves with love and compassion as we go through the dance of life. We lessen the intensity of our dramas as we learn to become non-judgmental witnesses. For example, if you start to lose your temper, watch yourself lose your temper, and think to yourself, Oh there I go losing my temper. *Hmm. That's interesting.* Wonder why I'm getting so upset.

If you lose your keys three times in two hours, misplace your wallet, spill coffee on your clothes, stop and think, *Hmm, that's interesting.* Wonder why I'm so scattered. If you continually go on spending sprees, say *Hmm, that's interesting* as you walk mesmerized through the store, buying things you don't need.

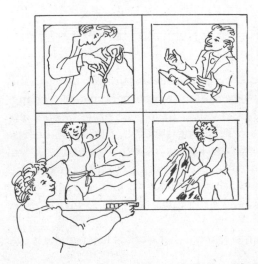

By watching yourself and saying *Hmm, that's interesting,* you raise your awareness to a *reflective* stance. Instead of feeling shame you experience fascination as you watch your life unfold. Creative solutions for life's struggle are more likely to emerge from this place of lighthearted reflection. This approach implies there are no mistakes, only experiments that work to one degree or another which help us feel free to take risks and try new ventures.

This approach is extremely helpful when you have contradictory dialogues going on in your head. "I want to go on a weekend vacation, but I should go visit my father." By saying *hmm, that's interesting* to each side and listening with genuine interest, you become the mediator to your own inner conflicts. Mediation always starts with understanding each side of a conflict—the motivations, the desires, and the goals. When we listen to ourselves in this caring, nonjudgmental way, we lower our inner turmoil and more easily make decisions.

Gently observing yourself applies to successes as well. If you are getting a first-place ribbon, giving a terrific talk, or just landed a great new job, you can also say, "*Hmm, that's interesting.* I'm good at this. This is fun. I'm glad this is happening." It's fine to be proud of yourself and feel happy. Success is also part of your drama, yet it means nothing about your essential worth as a human being.

16. EVERYONE IS RUNNING OFF THEIR PROGRAMMING, INCLUDING YOU

Each of us is a mystical, magical combination of our genetic, cultural, and family programming, which is constantly changing. Many of our beliefs and values have been *programmed* into us, but joy comes from realizing that we can change these teachings, we can choose the beliefs that feel right instead of being driven by unconscious conditioning. (This concept was core to the training I did at the Ken Keyes Center many years ago. It changed my life, and I have passed it on to many of my clients.)

When we think someone is terrific, it's because he or she meets our ideals; we like their belief system and their style of doing things. When we don't like someone, it's because he or she doesn't meet our ideals. Once we realize that it's all conditioning, however, we don't have to think of people as bad or wrong just because we don't like the way they are. You can intensely dislike someone's personality and behavior and still remember that that person is a sacred being just as you are; you can decide that you don't want to spend time with someone, but you don't have to throw that person out of your heart.

You can also use this concept on yourself. If you handle a situation unskillfully, say something inappropriate, or constantly get scared or depressed, you can say to yourself, "I am acting out *my* programming. It may not be useful programming, but I am not bad. I can learn to change it."

Remember, your programming isn't your core identity. Your beliefs and programming dance around the edges of your spirit, which is always sacred and always within you.

17. A BELIEF IS A BELIEF IS A BELIEF . . . BUT IT'S NOT NECESSARILY SO

It's fine to have beliefs and feel passionately about them so long as you remember that they are just beliefs and they are not necessarily right. Martha Boesing, a friend and playwright, once commented, "The biggest addiction, and one we least often talk about, is being addicted to beliefs. We really get hooked into thinking what we believe is true and right."

When your self-identity and beliefs merge, differences feel threatening. You are likely to defend your turf, become righteous and angry, and possibly shame or abuse other people who see things differently. When people adopt a belief—be it about religion, politics, sex roles, or whatever—as the one, correct belief, their minds get locked up in a rigid box, and other people with differing beliefs are

seen as the enemy. And what do you do to the enemy? Abuse them, shame them, hate them, or even kill them.

This doesn't mean you should put away your soap box if there is something important you want to say to the world. But if you *know* that "a belief is a belief is a belief" and it isn't necessarily so, you'll deliver your message in a way that more people can hear. And you will end up with a sense of humor. Righteous people are usually deadly serious. If you want an example, listen to the preachers on TV and wait for someone to laugh at himself or herself.

To feel joy is to have a capacity to hear others and be interested in their differences rather than afraid or threatened by them. This is part of being a mature person. We all have something to learn from others, be it about culture, religion, medicine, politics, or sex roles. Imagine how our world would be different if all children were taught about different religions in the world as different belief systems. Muslims *believe*, Christians *believe*, Jehovah's Witnesses *believe*, Pagans *believe*, Jews *believe*, Atheists *believe*. Imagine if all children were taught the different customs of different cultures and told that goodness is about tolerance, understanding, and compassion and that we can have love and respect for people who are different.

When I work with "recovering" Catholics or Fundamentalists who had been taught that their religion is the one and only right way, I try to help them understand that their beliefs *feel* true because they were indoctrinated very strongly at a vulnerable age. "You'll burn in hell if you don't do it this way" is a strong incentive to a five-year-old to adopt a belief.

So listen to your beliefs, think about how you learned them, and realize that they are not genetic, nor are they the "only way." You are free to acquire new perspectives, to absorb new ideas, and to question everything you were taught to believe. As your mind opens to exploration and change, you'll feel a new lightness and more joy.

18. YOU CAN BE RIGHT OR YOU CAN BE CLOSE

A core step to finding joy is connecting with other people. This can often involve bridging differences, with our partners, close friends, family, community, even other cultures. Most of us know how satisfying it can be when someone says, "You're right." And there is nothing wrong with that.

But when we get invested in proving that *we are right* and *others are wrong*, we break the web that connects us as humans.

When we take the stance that our way is the only way, we end up alone on a perch looking down on others. Sometimes, others who believe just as we do join us on the perch, but when we surround ourselves with people just like ourselves we don't grow or expand.

The dance of life involves learning to hang on to your heartfelt beliefs while respecting others' beliefs. It's fine to respectfully disagree without trying to change the other person. That way, everyone wins. Unfortunately, our culture perpetuates the model of win–lose in sports, the legal system, and schools. It's no wonder people carry the right–wrong approach into intimate relationships, often with negative results.

Working with couples, it is easy for me to see how being

attached to being right can erode a relationship. People argue over *the right way* to do things: "But the top sheet is supposed to go right side up." "How could you use soap in an iron skillet?" "You don't want to hang that picture *there!*" "How can you respect yourself living in such a sloppy house?" "It's so stupid to get the kids all excited just before bedtime." It helps if we realize that most of our beliefs come from the customs of our parents. Our beliefs seem "right" because we've adhered to them for so long, but this doesn't mean they *are* right. When we go from believing right–wrong thinking to simply stating our preferences and realizing that being right is not as wonderful as being close, we can let go of our demands, let things be, and return to joy.

My father was brought up to believe that arguing was a basic form of communication. I believe he truly cared about me and wanted us to have a good relationship, but whenever I came home with news of what I had learned in school or was excited about an idea, he would immediately argue with me. "How do you know that's right? What's your proof?" I hated it because he would never *share* in my joy. Instead of listening to me, he wanted me to prove my case. I felt as if I was being battered with logic. What he didn't understand was that the connection he wanted would have come from just listening and saying, "Oh, I'm glad to see you're excited. Tell me more about what you learned. Great. *Hmm.*"

Lively discourse can be wonderful. When we bring our creativity together and play with ideas in the spirit of finding the best solution for everyone, discussions can be fun, expansive, and intimate. It's far different than slugging people over the head with your beliefs.

When people want to argue with the goal of proving you wrong you may start to feel trapped and invaded. I certainly do. I've learned to say, "I don't want to argue with you." If the person goads you to engage in an argument, you can simply say, "I prefer not to debate the subject. Let's just respectfully disagree."

There is an Indian saying: "Don't judge a person until you have walked a mile in their moccasins." It is a freeing experience to suspend your judgments, let go of demands, and imagine yourself in the shoes of another. It expands our understanding, leads to compassion, and helps us become closer to one another.

19. THE AUTHORITIES AREN'T ALWAYS RIGHT (OR, REMEMBER GALILEO)

While it is important to let go of righteousness and become open to the beliefs and ideas of others, it is equally important to remember that just because someone speaks from a position of authority it doesn't mean he or she is right. If you have a belief that sings clearly in your heart, based on evidence that seems obvious to you, remember Galileo, and don't wait for the authorities to tell you you are right.

About Galileo: Roughly four hundred years ago he came to the conclusion that the earth was round and moved around the sun. This was considered heresy because common knowledge supposed that the earth was flat and that the sun and stars all moved around the earth. So Galileo was banned from teaching and taken to jail. But even as he walked out of the hearing where the judge and jury found him guilty, he muttered to himself that the earth did move around the sun.

If we look historically at medical practices, attitudes toward sex, nutrition information, school rules, religious beliefs, and all institutions, we will see that beliefs and habits change. Remember: George Washington bled to death from the common medical practice of bleeding people when they were sick with the flu; parents were told to feed babies only every four hours; people were taught they would go crazy if they masturbated; until the 1980s, people who believed nutrition was linked to health were considered weird, and now most magazines routinely run articles on diets for good health. *So remember, what you are told is good for you may have more to do with customs and politics than a heartfelt interest in your well-being. Think for yourself.*

I have long believed in using all forms of natural healing whenever possible. When I had breast cancer a few years ago, I had extensive Reiki healing before, during, and after my surgery (*Reiki* means "life force energy" and is a method of channeling a high vibration of light energy into the body, which ignites one's natural healing power.) I had spoken to my surgeon about it. After coming out of the anesthetic, the surgeon came in and asked if I had had a shot for pain. I said, "No. I wasn't having much pain due to the Reiki," and she said, "You'll have more pain tomorrow." The next day the doctor and nurse were amazed that I could lift my arm straight up and reach around my back and button a blouse. But when I tried to explain how Reiki healing helped me, their eyes glazed over. When people are trained to believe in one discipline it's as if channels in the brain that might consider alternatives get blocked off.

So did I stop doing Reiki healing? Of course not. I continue to quietly mention it to people because every now and then someone's eyes light up and they are interested in learning more. And that's wonderful because I'm hoping one day that anyone having surgery or illness could have Reiki or some form of channeled healing to ease the pain and speed recovery.

Even in the face of the "latest research," the doctor's orders, the philosophy of your religion, ask yourself: What do I believe? What makes sense? What works? *And then try it out.* And be willing to change your conclusions when you have evidence that suggests differently. Let your body, mind, and spirit be your guide. But don't expect the experts to hear you or agree with you if you disagree with their rules. The Galileo syndrome is still alive and well. The other fascinating part of this saga is that it took the Catholic Church four hundred years to pardon Galileo. (Mind you—they didn't apologize, they only pardoned him. I think they should have sent flowers to his grave.)

The morals of this story:

- Don't wait for someone's permission to believe yourself.
- Check out all belief systems in the context of politics, religion, and custom.
- When you are handed a rule, ask yourself, Who benefits by this rule?
- Don't do anything that doesn't feel right or insults your soul.
- Remember Galileo.

20. WHATEVER ANYONE SAYS OR DOES MEANS NOTHING ABOUT YOUR WORTH

A great deal of my work as a psychologist centers on helping people realize that other people's opinions of them are simply opinions that come through their own filter. In other words, whatever anyone says does means nothing, absolutely nothing, about your worth as a human being. A person may give you useful feedback, have something valuable to say, but whether they like you, approve of you, or admire you need not affect your sense of worth or self-esteem. If everyone could internalize this belief, we could all relax and enjoy the show—the snow, the rain, the great big picture of life. We are free to feel joy when our self-worth rests quietly within us, not on the lips of others.

Unfortunately, many people live as if their self-esteem had a cord connecting them to external events and people. You receive praise, someone says you're nice or sends you a valentine

and your self-esteem goes up. You don't pass your driver's test, you get fired, someone is rude to you, your best friend forgets your birthday and your self-esteem goes down. This is the essence of a victim stance; you think the world is doing it to you. While you may have been victimized in your life, you are not a victim. You have a mind that can operate on your behalf by saying over and over, *Whatever anyone says means nothing about my worth.*

The goal is to observe what others say to you as you would a leaf on a tree. The wonderful thing about being a group therapist is constantly seeing how each person's history affects his or her interpretation of a situation. Recently, in response to how I handled a situation, two people thought I was mean, three thought I was caring, two were confused, and another was thinking about lunch and never heard the interaction.

An analogy that is sometimes useful is imagining that someone throws a dart at your arm. It cuts your skin, you bleed, and it stings. That's a given. But you always have a choice about what you say to your heart and soul. You can hurt yourself further by saying: "He threw a dart at me. What did I do to deserve this? What did I do wrong? I must be a jerk and a bad person." Or you can also be kind to yourself by saying: "Ouch, that person threw a dart, that's not nice, that hurts. I'd better get out of here and get a Band-Aid and stay away from people who throw darts."

So if you want to save money on stress-related problems and counseling, simply say the phrase over and over a couple of hundred times a day until it sinks in: *Whatever anyone says or does means nothing about my worth.* Once this phrase lives within you it will help free that magical, musical instrument that is your soul, so you can laugh and sing and stop worrying about what everyone thinks about you (because usually, they're not thinking about you at all: they might be wondering what you are thinking of them . . . or about how to get the bills paid, or whether to have another cup of coffee).

21. SPEND A DAY SAYING, "THAT'S JUST THE WAY I AM"

Like endless static on a radio blocking a person from hearing the music, many people have a tape recorder in their head barraging them with messages such as, "I messed up again." "I'm too loud." "I'm too slow." "I'm too fat." "I'll never find the right job." "I'll always be alone."

A powerful antidote to such self-defeating talk is to stop, STOP, think of yourself just as you are this moment, and say to yourself, *"That's just the way I am. I am as I am."* If you have things you tend to regret in yourself, try making some "That's just the way I am" statements. Here are some examples:

- "I get anxious filling out IRS forms. *That's just the way I am.*"
- "I get scared and don't stand up for myself. *That's just the way I am.*"
- "I wear a size-6 top and size-12 slacks. *That's just the way I am.*"
- "Sometimes I interrupt. *That's just the way I am.*"

Sometimes at workshops I have people pair up and do this exercise. One makes a *"That's just the way I am"* statement and the other repeats it back in a nonchalant way.

"I get terribly hard on myself when I make mistakes and *that's just the way I am.*"

The partner replies, "You get terribly hard on yourself when you make mistakes, and *that's just the way you are.*"

This process has a tremendous ability to help people become less intense about their foibles, because it makes them seem less serious.

While it's important not to use this statement as justification for harming someone, it is a powerful tool in learning to accept yourself. The Course in Miracles has a saying, "I am as God created me." I would add to this: "I am as I am *this minute.* I'd like to change, and maybe I can, but for whatever reason, this is where I am standing on my journey today." And the more you can simply accept this moment on your journey and realize it is part of a great mystery, the more you will cease the negative rattling in your mind.

In a certain therapy group where nearly everyone had lived with a constant barrage of self-defeating messages in their head, I had each person say out loud everything that was going on. It became a can-you-top-this sort of conversation, and we ended up laughing until we cried, because it suddenly sounded so ridiculous. "No, I'm more of a jerk than you." "No, I say more stupid things." "I'm always worrying what people think." "I'm thirty-five and I don't have a career." "No. No. I've messed up worse than you. I was part of an escort service." "No. No. I'm worse, I shoplifted." "I'm the worst. I hate my mother and I've hit my child." It was wonderfully freeing to throw all the mental cacophony out in the room, like an orchestra warming up. It was as if everyone dumped the garbage out of their head, leaving room for more joyful thoughts.

After the big shame and guilt dump, one woman mentioned the "Saturday Night Live" TV show, which parodies the self-help movement by having someone stand in front of a mirror and say (in a syrupy way), "I'm good enough, I'm smart enough, and doggone it, people like me." So we adopted that phrase in the group, and when people started railing on themselves we'd say, "Doggone it, I like you," or "That's just the way you are." And usually, we'd all start laughing at ourselves. What a good way to move toward joy.

TAPPING THE POWER
OF YOUR MIND
A Training Manual for the Brain

22. YOU HAVE MORE POWER
WHEN YOU THINK

If there is such a thing as magic it is our ability to change our emotional and physical state simply by changing our thoughts. One night I came back to my car after seeing a movie and saw that the window was smashed. I was immediately upset. My heart started pounding and my stomach was churning. Then I remembered that I had my tape recorder and tape collection in the back seat and I was more upset. I opened the back door and much to my surprise saw that the tape recorder and tapes were still there. Immediately my heart rate slowed down, I felt intensely happy over my good fortune of having *only* a broken window. Within two minutes' time I had a completely different response to the broken window. It was all related to my thoughts.

We've been given this incredible organ called the brain, but we aren't handed a user's manual. We get better directions when we buy a can opener or a washing machine. The brain can be our ally for enjoying life and creating joy, rather than a remote-control message machine that often taunts us, haunts us, and sometimes seems like a robot inside, controlling our lives.

Thoughts and words direct energy throughout the body. For example, if you repeatedly say to yourself, "People *should* be nice to me at all times." "Computers *shouldn't* break down," or "Something is wrong with *me*," you will probably be upset, feel heavy, and bring gloom to your relationships. If, on the other hand, you accept that the dance of life includes people making thoughtless remarks, computers having blowouts, cats scratching on your new carpet, and getting laid off from your job, you will probably feel lighter, have more energy, and transmit welcoming signals to friends and loved ones. You'll also help your immune system, blood count, and energy level. This may sound simple-minded, but it works—just like turning on a light helps you to see better. (Many people have made fun of Norman Vincent Peale's *The Power of Positive Thinking*. But millions of copies have been sold over the years, and we've come to know he was right, kind of like Galileo.)

It may seem to you that feelings of anger, sadness, or shame attack you like a sudden rainstorm. But it's all about what's going on in your head. *Here's a short list of examples to help jog your mind:*

- Shame follows saying "I'm defective. I'm unlovable."
- Despair follows saying "Life is hopeless. There's nothing I can do about it."
- Fear follows saying "She's got to like me. I'm nothing without her."
- Anger follows saying "That person *should* do it my way."
- Violence and righteous indignation often follow thinking "I can't live without her. How dare she do that to me. I'll show her who's boss."

If you want to experience the power of your mind, take a couple of deep breaths, release them slowly, and tune into your body. Then say the following to yourself, absorbing the meaning of each statement unto your whole being:

No matter what I have done, I deserve respect—always and forever.
No matter whether I make mistakes, I am worthy of love.
No matter what my looks or skills, I am a worthwhile person.

Hold on to these images. Tell yourself they are true. Do you feel different? If you do, that's because of your thoughts. Nothing else changed while you practiced these affirmations.

23. YOU CAN BE LATE AND UPSET OR YOU CAN SIMPLY BE LATE

Once you realize that by changing your thoughts you can change your feelings, it's time to practice. Have you ever become anxious, frustrated, or afraid on your way to a gathering or meeting of some sort because you knew you'd be late? Stop for a moment and remember such a situation. Bring the image to your mind. You might be stuck in traffic, on a subway, or in an airplane, or you might be in bed just realizing you slept through your alarm. Then say to yourself: "*There is absolutely nothing I can do to get there sooner. I can be late and upset or I can simply be late.* I can sit in this car/bus/train/plane and be friendly to the people around me, look at the leaves/clouds/patterns in the pavement, or I can raise my blood pressure, be a pain in the neck to others, and stress my body gripping the steering wheel, getting indignant, blaming myself or other people. *I have a choice.* Being riled up will not help one bit in getting to my destination on time."

You can use this type of thinking in hundreds of situations. Simply imagine your head as a radio station, and change the channel from the It's-a-catastrophe station to the It's-just-a-nuisance station. I think of the computer expression Garbage In, Garbage Out—you can apply this to your mind as well.

Here are a few examples to use for changing the channel of your mind; substitute a line in the second column for any in the first column:

Garbage In, Garbage Out	
Changing the Channels of your Mind	
Words That Upset	Words That Bring Balance
It's a catastrophe.	It's only a pain in the neck.
It's terrible.	It's a disappointment.
It's awful.	It's a nuisance.
It shouldn't be that way.	That's life, that's the way things are.
I can't stand it.	I *prefer* it to be different.
I'm devastated.	I'm sad—but I'll survive.
It's not fair/It should be fair.	Life is not fair.
I shouldn't make mistakes.	Everyone makes mistakes.
I can't stand this pain.	It hurts but it won't last forever. This too shall pass.

The more you make these substitutions, the more you relax your body, feel a sense of control, and become closer to joy.

24. AFFIRMATIONS WORK . . . IF YOU SAY ENOUGH OF THEM

The principle of affirmations is that light energy crowds out dense energy. Dense energy comes from creating negative, self-defeating thoughts, and light energy comes from replacing negative thoughts with self-affirming thoughts that help you take charge of your life and move forward. You take an old, dense thought (I "*can't* take care of myself") and replace it with a lighter thought ("I *can* take care of myself," or "I *am learning* to take care of myself," or "I *can learn* to take care of myself"), and you say it thousands of times.

It's important to have affirmations that are short, pithy, and to the point. Statements like, "I can allow myself to develop traits that help me have good relationships" are too wordy. "I can learn to have friends" usually connects more deeply and comes from the part of us that understands simple words. When you find an affirmation that is right for you, you'll feel a sense of rightness in your gut.

Affirmations also feel phony if they are in direct opposition to what you are experiencing. For example, if you say, "I'm happy, content, and competent," when you feel miserable, worthless, and incompetent, it will feel hollow. I prefer affirmations that suggest the *possibility* of change. For example, "*I have the power to feel better.*" "*I can love myself by* eating healthy food." "*I am learning to* change my thoughts." These statements open up the path and don't clash so hard with our entrenched beliefs.

To add energy to an affirmation, add movement. You can dance it, sing it, tap it, make up a rhythm to go with it, run and say it while clicking on a lap counter. Do anything to get the message into your brain, through as many channels as possible. But don't give up if it doesn't happen right away. It takes a lot of repetition to overcome the density of old thought patterns.

I used to think that affirmations were a lot of corny, New Age stuff. But when I was completely stuck trying to write my first book, I started running twenty-five minutes a day carrying a lap counter, clicking it, while saying, "I can love myself by writing this book." At first it was easy. But after a couple of weeks my resistant side mounted a counterattack. I would feel exhausted in the morning, misplace my running shoes, or start thinking that this affirmation stuff was silly. This type of resistance is typical when an affirmation starts to threaten an unconscious belief. That's the time to sneak around the ego resistance and keep going. After two months the resistance decreased considerably. Then one day while running, it was as if the original affirmation "I can love myself by writing this book" dissolved into the word love and I felt a warm golden glow both around me and inside me. I felt completely peaceful and I knew with complete certainty that I could write my book. The repetition of the words had created a shift in consciousness.

When you assert your self-love by saying affirmations, a negative rebuttal may come up: "Oh no you can't. Who do you think you are?" or "Fat chance." These are probably phrases that someone else said or implied and triggered your negative patterns in the first place. You can observe them as peripheral chatter, breathe into them, or talk back to them: "I'm not going to take you seriously." "Oh that's just the voice of my parents/religion." However, allow only one rebuttal before repeating the affirmation.

If you want to do affirmations but feel a lot of resistance, you can say to yourself, "It will get easier after the first couple of days. I'll be much happier if I change this belief. Twenty-five

minutes four times a week is small potatoes in the course of a lifetime. And it's a lot cheaper than therapy." (The last thought has
been particularly helpful to me.)

25. DOUBLE YOUR POWER: GET A SELF-ESTEEM CHORUS

We've talked about harnessing your power as an individual to
change your thoughts and feelings. Belonging to a group of people pulling together, helps increase that power incredibly. One
way to do this is to invite some friends over for an evening to
play the Self-esteem Chorus game. I use this approach in therapy
groups and workshops, where we see the power of our energy
working together.

In one of my therapy groups was a woman, Jeanne, who was
taunted by the thoughts: "I'll never get what I want, so why ask
for it, and I'll be punished if I
ask for what I want. Nice girls
don't ask for what they
want—especially sex." With a
little brainstorming from the
group, she came up with a
single affirmation that countered her negative beliefs: "I
get to ask for what I want."
Then she stood in the center of
a circle and had each person
say to her, "You get to ask for
what you want." They could
whisper it in her ear, say it
seriously, sing it, whatever—
anything to get the message
through to her brain.

At first it felt a bit contrived and stiff. But as we went around the circle, one person started to say it with a rap rhythm, someone else started tapping, and we ended up with everyone tapping and dancing and saying it together, "You get to ask for what you want. Yeah ... yeah ... yeah ... yeah ... yeah." Over and over. It felt like a party, and the phrase has stuck in Jeanne's mind ever since ... (not to mention mine).

People have used the self-esteem chorus to be sung to and rocked like a child, to release the belief, "I'm bad," and to internalize the belief, "I'm lovable." One very touching experience occurred when a woman who was very ashamed of her dependency asked the self-esteem chorus to put their hands on her shoulders and say things like, "It's fine to have needs. Everyone has needs. We all want to be loved. You are lovable." Following these affirmations of her, one woman sang a lullaby.

It's important that everyone set up their scenario in their own special way. It's all right for others to make suggestions, but they must be offered in the spirit of helping the person find his or her own dance. It can be especially powerful when people are deeply tuned in and respond to the person in a creative way.

Having a group pull together to help each other is powerful, affirming, and makes space for all forms of creativity. It also helps people bond together, and is often a healing experience for all who take part. There is something empowering about a community of committed friends helping each other find their love and power.

26. UNDERSTANDING PAIRED ASSOCIATIONS (OR, WHY DO I GET SO ANXIOUS OVER COOKING, BALANCING A CHECKBOOK, ETC.?)

Most of us have some tasks or areas of life we avoid because they make us anxious. It can be balancing a checkbook, cooking, putting up a tent, playing the violin, raking leaves, going to a movie alone, thinking of sex, or phoning someone to ask for help. To help us move toward joy, it is important not to shame ourselves for these reactions but to understand their source and have some methods for changing them.

While we all have different types of learning styles and some projects will be more to our liking than others, a task that creates sudden anxiety often has its roots in an old experience in which an event and feelings got paired together.

For example, when Ellie wanted to try cooking, her mother was extremely compulsive about measuring everything perfectly and not spilling anything. She voiced sharp criticism at any mistakes. There was no creativity or joy. Ellie did learn how to cook, but, as an adult, when she pulled the cooking information out of her brain it was paired with the anxiety of being criticized. That's the principle of paired associations: when the learning is recalled, the accompanying emotions from the original learning situation are recalled as well.

As a piano teacher for many years, I've heard endless stories from people who quit lessons because they had to play in recitals. All year long, practicing piano was paired with the fear of having to perform by memory, an experience that triggered a nervous stomach, anxiety, and fear of having a memory slip. An old friend of mine, Frank, quit the violin after three lessons at the age of seven when his teacher said with disdain, "You have no talent." He has never picked up an instrument since then.

Another friend of mine, Jessie, who got profoundly anxious whenever she had to deal with money, tracked her emotions back to a childhood experience. Her parents didn't have enough money to pay the bills, so they sent their young daughter with partial payments, figuring no one would get angry at a small child. So Jessie carried the money, and the anxiety. I remember her face lighting up when she made the connection. She was able to laugh and say, "No wonder I'm so messed up with money."

Cultural sterotypes have a profound effect as well. I remember being fascinated with my father's wood shop as a child and he was very nice about showing me how he did things. But the cultural messages that omitted any image of women using a drill or a cross-cut saw prevailed. My response to picking up a drill was to feel suddenly anxious or afraid. Many years later when I bought a drill, I felt a sense of paralysis every time I thought of using it.

Some paired associations affect life in a much deeper way. In my work with male and female sexual abuse survivors, I see over and over how sexually derogatory remarks, incest, and sexual abuse create negative paired associations with sexuality. A person starts to be sexual and then gets anxious, panicky, or numb because sexuality is paired with violence, shame, betrayal, fear, disgust, rage, or sorrow. What's more upsetting is that the memories are often lodged in the unconscious mind, so the person is not aware of the source of the fears until they are unraveled in psychotherapy or with healing rituals.

So if you have some of these anxious responses, don't put yourself down. Remember to say, *Hmm. That's interesting. I wonder what it's all about.* Then backtrack and see if you can make a connection with events in your life.

27. OVERCOMING PAIRED ASSOCIATIONS: THAT WAS THEN, THIS IS NOW

So what can you do with strong automatic reactions that you feel are controlling you? Once you have tracked the root of a paired association, you can start retraining your mind. You can even retrain yourself without knowing the source.

First, stop putting yourself down and saying, "I can't." Start saying things like:

- It's something I learned.
- It's not about being stupid.
- It's not my fault.
- I'm not bad.
- It's a drag but not a catastrophe.
- It happens to people all the time.
- I can change it.

Another phrase many people find helpful is *That was then, this is now. I can do it differently.* You may need to say this over and over.

Frank, who was told he had no talent for the violin, decided as an adult to take violin lessons. He lessened his anxiety by saying, "It was wrong of that teacher to say I had no talent. *That was then, this is now.* Maybe I won't be great, but I could enjoy taking violin lessons." He found a teacher who was sensitive to his fears. When the voice of his old teacher paid a visit, he would say, "I'm not going to listen to you anymore. I'm going to play." As he practiced, he still had some of the anxiety, but it no longer controlled him, and with time it slowly faded.

I once taught a course on performance anxiety for pianists. We made it a party atmosphere. People played pieces at half speed, deliberately made their hands tremble (which is almost impossible to do), tripped walking up to perform, played pieces as badly as they could, and forgot the notes in the middle and turned to the group to say, "I forgot and you'd better be nice to me." We also talked about the worst-case scenario if you got up and performed badly. Would you die? Go hungry? Be flogged by a friend? This helped put the whole situation in perspective. We did things to get people laughing, to help them separate their performance from their self-worth. The students started to associate piano playing with laughter, sharing their vulnerability in a safe way, and learning that mistakes are not catastrophes.

Another way to break a paired association is to replay an experience with a caring person. Ellie decided to relieve her cooking anxiety by having a friend who enjoyed cooking come over and cook with her. On one occasion she invited several friends to cook together, followed by a candlelight dinner. The feelings associated with cooking changed from anxiety to fun, creativity, and pleasure.

For my own paired association with the power drill, after six months of taking it out and putting it back, I finally held it in my hand, yelled out loud, "I am going to do this!" plugged it in, pulled the trigger, and installed a doorbell. It was great—one more thing not to be afraid of. One more part of me freed up for joy.

(Changing sexual responses is more complex and takes more time, but it involves essentially the same process. A detailed explanation is not within the scope of this book, but I talk about it at length in *Women, Sex, and Addiction: A Search for Love and Power*. Wendy Maltz has also written a book on this subject, *The Sexual Healing Journey*.)

Some people don't want to bother overcoming these anxieties;

they feel they can just avoid the situation that triggers them. And that's true in many situations. However, in breaking through old patterns, we release fear, expand our self-definition, and send a message to our whole being that we have the power to change and create joy.

28. RESEARCH YOUR ASSUMPTIONS

Sometimes we adopt certain beliefs when we're children and use them automatically when we become adults, without ever checking them out against reality. This brings to mind the story of the woman who always cut off the end of the turkey when she put it in the oven. Her daughter asked her why, and her mother responded, "I don't know. My mother always did it." Then she went and asked her mother, who said, "I don't know. My mother always did it." She went and asked her mother, who said, "The oven wasn't big enough."

As we clear our mind to make way for joy, we need to examine the ways we shrink our lives with assumptions. For example, a woman in one of my therapy groups rarely ate out with friends because she thought people were staring at her. We took her fear apart. The first question was, What are the possible reasons people might stare at her? The group brainstormed: Because she looks great. Because she is attractive. Because she is unusual. So a stare could be a compliment as well as a negative response, and one would never know. Then we suggested she go to a restaurant with some friends, look around, and count the people who were staring at her. She did so and found it to be anticlimactic. One person glanced at her, and no one else even turned their head.

So research the little statements like, People won't like me if I. . . . Everyone will think I'm bad for. . . . I'll hurt someone if I. . . . You may find out it's only your fear talking, to stop you from speaking the truth or taking risks. So try examining these phrases and researching your thoughts. Living in reality is freeing and helps us on our journey toward joy.

29. EMBRACE THE DANCE OF CHANGE

Change is exciting but scary—it usually involves letting go of loyalty to a belief, which is attached to loyalty to a person. For example, if my father told me I was stupid, believing I'm intelligent can unconsciously feel like being disloyal to my father. When we believe we are inferior, powerless, lack ability, or need someone to take care of us, it can feel like we're committing a crime against *the Gods/parents/authority figures* to say "I can take control. I can change my life. I can learn something new. I can create happiness." Some people experience intense guilt when they assert their autonomy. But guilt is only a form of withdrawal that comes when you dare to expand your limits.

Don't get discouraged when you start acting on your behalf and some voices of the past loom large in your mind, threatening you with dire consequences for the crime of moving toward wholeness. The voices might say: You'll get in trouble, go to hell, or have an accident. Or, you're being arrogant, selfish, uppity, wimpy, brazen, bitchy, unlovable, whatever. It's important not to give up during these times but rather to keep going in the face of this internal censor.

I had an intense conflict with my internal censor when I joined a chorale, a fulfillment of a long-time dream, particularly because they were going to sing my favorite work, the *German Requiem* of Brahms. The conductor didn't have time to try me out but took me because I had taught piano and had sung in a choir. I was relieved he accepted me without a tryout, but at the first rehearsal my internal censor taunted me: You don't belong here; you don't sing as well as the others (I was sitting beside a voice major). Images of singing a note loudly during a rest danced in my mind.

After a few rehearsals I had a dream that the conductor called me and in a solemn voice said, "Charlotte, people have been reporting you for missing notes, and we can't have that. I'll have to ask you to leave." I woke up in a cold sweat . . . but I kept going to rehearsals. To boost my confidence, I took voice lessons and practiced frequently. Then I got a bronchial cough the week before the performance. I finally succumbed to taking antibiotics and my cough cleared up. Then the day of the performance I got scattered trying to get dressed and was nearly late because I couldn't decide which earrings to wear (as if it mattered). When I got in the car I was plagued with the thought that I'd have an accident on the way to the concert, and I nearly did. But, finally, finally, there I was standing on the riser amid three hundred musicians, filled with joy, singing this glorious music that touches my soul.

When we push through limitations, our unconscious censor can play havoc with us. But persevere. There is joy on the other side. The censor is only a paper dragon in your mind. Your parents aren't in the room, neither is the mean teacher you had in second grade, the person who abused you, or the pope. You are free to think, expand, dream, create visions of happiness and fulfill them.

30. ACCEPT YOURSELF, REMEMBERING AND FORGETTING

You get on the path of exercising, saying affirmations, writing regularly, paying the bills on time, not criticizing your partner, and then, . . . yikes! You revert to old behavior. You can't seem to drag yourself out to exercise, you start carping at your partner, you gorge on food. In short, you forget to do all the things that are good for you.

On the path to joy, it is important to accept that we wax and wane like the moon. We remember, we forget—and it's all part of the dance. We push through our fears, get organized, take a risk, then retreat for a while. After a break, we once again push through inertia, and get going again.

Remember, you never have to do anything perfectly. Four affirmations are better than none. Walking once a week is better than once a month. Fresh vegetables three times a week is better than an unmitigated junk food diet.

Sometimes people get into binge-and-starve cycles, attempting to make multiple changes all at once only to find out that their system can handle only so much change at a time. At one point, I stuck to my resolution not to eat fat and sugar, exercised every day, wrote every day, cleared out tons of junk from the basement, returned all my phone calls on time . . . and started to get very sad. My chest and throat tightened up, and I started to feel sick. Then when my roommate sat beside me in bed and rubbed my chest with a healing cream, I heard myself say as I started to cry, "It's so hard to love yourself more than you've been loved!" Then I got bronchitis.

So if you fall off the track, get up and try again. Tell yourself you get to love yourself. Find a balance: nudge yourself, practice, yet be gentle. If you slip on your diet and eat a banana split, eat it slowly while savoring every bite, then breathe deeply and cook some brown rice. If life is getting chaotic, don't get hysterical, pick up one thing and do it. If you have an anxiety attack and pull your covers over your head for a while, enjoy the cocoon. If you had been keeping your room organized and it suddenly looks like a trash heap, start sorting papers again, or decide to take a week off and let the clutter rest, and then ask a friend to help you get reorganized.

The important thing is to watch yourself play the remembering and forgetting game and be gentle at all times. How you fall off the path is part of the path. It's easy to love yourself when you're winning. The real test is maintaining that love on the tough days. So keep remembering (until you forget) that it's all drama, it's all a dance, and it's all okay.

LIGHTEN UP
Finding Balance in a Crazy World

31. IT MATTERS, BUT IT'S NOT SERIOUS

Having balance in our lives helps us find joy. Keeping our equilibrium is about letting things matter yet realizing they are probably not of earth-shaking seriousness.

People who get lost in the "it matters" side of the equation tend to treat every little ache, slight, upset, mistake, or rejection as if they qualify for headline news. Someone slights them and they hold on to it, chew on it, bear grudges, or get obsessed with it. On the other hand, people who don't let anything matter tend to grin and bear it, numb out natural feelings, and say "It's fine" even when their best friend betrays them, the roof leaks, or their feet ache.

Both of these approaches leave out part of the picture. If you tend to create a big drama about life's bumps, you might want to develop your ability to realize that it's not terribly serious—it's only a cosmic blink in time. On the other hand, if you tend to tough out situations and play the martyr, you might want to give yourself permission to let things matter a lot more. Let yourself feel your anger, jealousy, sadness, frustration, hurt, or resentment.

One way to balance the two concepts is to first let it matter! When something upsetting happens, let yourself feel the disappointment. Don't swallow it. Don't rationalize it. Feel it. Otherwise, it festers away inside. Then, after you have had a good fit or a good whine, back off and put the experience or problem in perspective. Look at the big picture. Find a phrase that brings you back to yourself, and puts things in perspective. (I remind myself that I have shelter, a warm bed, food, friends, and work, and the rest is gravy.) Then write it down and put it up someplace so it will be there when you need it. The more we accept our inner world and the less we deny, the more we come home to our center and the dwelling place of our joy.

32. REMIND YOURSELF: WHAT IS, IS

Once when I went to a spiritual counselor hoping for some profound words of wisdom, she told me to say, *What is, is,* one hundred times a day. Sixty dollars for this, I thought. But you know, it *was* magical and life changing because it helped me accept the moment and stop fighting with myself. *What is, is. I'm tired.* No arguing with it, just the simple recognition of what is. *What is, is. I just got bumped off a plane and will sit in this airport for six hours.*

What is, is, I just dented my car. What is, is, my partner is late. What is, is, I'm angry. What is, is, I'm nervous about this job interview. What is, is, I'm lonely. What is, is, I'm happy and content. It's just what is. It's the truth, it's where my life is right this moment. It's not good, it's not bad, it's just what's happening at the moment.

Saying *What is, is,* helps us stop demanding that situations and people be different. It also allows us to drop into our feelings, which connects us to our inner wisdom. So often people will say,

I'm upset with my partner, *but* . . . I know he's under a lot of pressure. They start to see truth and then, because it's uncomfortable, they interrupt themselves with a rationalization and never find out how they really feel about it. Once we let ourselves acknowledge *What is, is,* and just sit with it and have our feelings, we can make decisions about what we want to do about it. Do I like this situation, do I want to stay or go? Is there something I could do to change it?

Reminding ourselves, *what it is,* leads us to joy because it aligns us with the truth, and the truth is like a river of spirit that flows through the dramas of life connecting us back to our source.

33. ADOPT A COSMIC PERSPECTIVE: KEEP YOUR SPIRIT ALIVE IN POLLUTION

Recently, when I flew over the mountains in Oregon and Montana and saw huge, clear-cut areas of the forests like huge, raw wounds on a sleeping giant, it seemed as if the earth were dying, its immune system being poisoned and

destroyed. I felt sharp pangs of grief and anger.

So I sat for a while feeling overwhelming grief. Then I decided I wanted to shift my mood. So I applied a cosmic perspective to *What is, is.* I said to myself: The planet earth has a life span of eight billion years, give or take a few million. People have been around for approximately forty thousand years—a virtual blink in the cosmos. It is sad that we as a species are ravaging the natural world so fast that we are jeopardizing our survival. If we wipe ourselves out, it would be the height of folly, but the earth will survive even us. It will eventually restore itself. It might take a few thousand years, and it won't be just as it was before, but its life is stronger than death.

As I thought this, I felt myself relax. I pictured something green growing back in the empty places. I thought of the rivers finally being clean again, certainly not in my lifetime and possibly not with any people around, but I knew that one day in the great big picture it would be all right.

While I care passionately about what happens to our planet, I can care and be upset or I can care and be relaxed. And if I relax I'll have more energy to help make changes.

34. REMEMBER YOU ARE NOT ALONE

Here is a technique to use if your current struggles seem very big and you feel alone or overwhelmed. Imagine flying up above the earth, looking down, and pretending you can see into people's homes, hospitals, office buildings, and schools. Observe all the events going on: someone is practicing the violin, a child is being born, a man is dying of cancer, a couple is making love, a boy is being sung to, an old woman is sitting alone in a nursing home, hoping her daughter will come visit, a family is having a reunion, a man on a diet is eating fudge. The drama goes on for everyone, and we are a part of it all.

You may think you're the only one alone on a Saturday night, but you're not. Everyone deals with loss, aging, loneliness. Too often we get lost in a given moment and forget that we are not alone. We are connected to a huge web of life, and most people experience the feelings we are feeling. So if you are lonely, be lonely, but don't tell yourself you are alone.

35. TUNE INTO ENERGY

Bright, dull, cold, earthy, warm, fiery, heavy, and *sleazy* are words we use to describe the essence of people, their energy field. When we meet someone, we respond to their physical appearance and to the energy they transmit. Albert Einstein taught us that everything is an energy vibration: $E = mc^2$ (energy equals matter times the speed of light squared). This means that everything is moving, everything is alive, everything is vibrating—wood, plants, bricks, and people. If you don't totally comprehend this formula at an intellectual level, you probably do know what it's like to meet someone who's "on the same wave-

length" or a "kindred spirit." You know what it's like to be attracted to a particular color or hear sounds that are pleasing.

When my daughter was little she said to me, "I always know just when Ralph [the cat] is going to come around the corner of the house." That's because she could pick up his energy field. Many people who go into their home after it has been robbed have an immediate sense that something is wrong, even though they see nothing at first. They are picking up the energy field of their home, which has been violated.

Have you ever met someone and felt uplifted, nurtured, and happy just being around them? Have you ever met a person and had an instant, negative, almost sick reaction, particularly if they touch you? You are feeling their energy get inside you.

Tuning into energy and trusting our perceptions is empowering because it gives us much richer information about people and situations. For example, if someone says he will phone you but averts his eyes and speaks in a glib way or with a dull voice, don't count on hearing from him.

Sensing energy means looking at people's eyes, listening to the sound of their voice, and letting yourself sense the tone of their presence. It also means listening to your body's reaction. If you constantly get a knot in your stomach or lose energy being around someone, you are probably picking up something about that person on an unconscious level. You may be sensing that the words and behavior don't match.

Often when I help clients backtrack and look for the red flags that should have signaled they were getting into an abusive or difficult relationship, they say, "Oh, yes, I had a weird feeling about that, but I thought it meant something was wrong with me." Listen to those weird feelings. Try to name them, talk about them, and trust them. Part of experiencing joy is feeling confident that we can take care of ourselves and be wise in attracting people to us. When we develop the ability to trust our gut—our energy readings—we are much safer and happier.

36. LEARN TO TAKE ENERGY READINGS: A THERMOMETER FOR SELF-PRESERVATION

Here is how you can use energy readings on everything in your life—food, books, magazines, TV shows, clothes, places you walk to, organizations you belong to, the way you create your living space.

To take an energy reading, imagine a thermometer inside you going from light to dense on a scale of 1 to 10. When you consider spending time with a friend, reading a book, selecting food, making love, buying clothes, interviewing for a job, looking at a new apartment, simply take a reading on a scale of 1 to 10 of how light or dense you feel. It's amazing how most people come up with a number right away.

If a scale of 1 to 10 doesn't work for you, simply ask yourself, Do I feel light, nurtured, positive, energized? Or do I feel heavy, dense, dull, and lethargic? This doesn't mean we always avoid struggle or challenge, but we develop a concept of ourselves as an energy field. We need to create a balance between taking in and giving out. We could think of self-love as taking good care of your energy field—going where the energy helps you feel lighter and not getting drained or overloaded. The more we live by this measure of our inner truth, the more energy we have because we operate from inner wisdom instead of conditioning.

If your energy is heavy, find out where you put your mental attention. If you focus on pain and misery, you might experiment by thinking of the positive things in your life; talk about them with others, and notice their reaction as well as your own energy level.

We are sometimes faced with having to choose between conflicting energy responses. For example, you look at a menu and your taste buds jump with joy at the thought of pasta with cream sauce, wine, and the double brownie delight. The other part of you has a dense energy reading from thinking: But what about afterward? I'll feel heavy. I might not sleep so well. The fat will go to my hips. Once I'm full it won't have made any difference. So we dance between the two impulses and hopefully reach for the joy that is most likely to feed our spirit and bring happiness in the long run.

37. DEATH IS PART OF LIFE

It may seem strange to talk about death in a book on joy. But freeing ourselves to find joy also involves making peace with the concept of death, something we all will face. It doesn't mean you become perfectly comfortable with it. It means you let yourself feel your discomfort or fear or fascination and ponder the mystery.

Our culture avoids talking about natural death and is obsessed with violent death. Yet people who work with the dying are some of the most peaceful people I have known. Perhaps it's because they do not flee from facing this important aspect of life. A group of people in Missoula, Montana (the Chalice of Repose), who minister to the dying with music and loving care, recently gave a harp

and choral concert in a historic Catholic church that had incredible, colorful, rococo paintings covering the walls and ceiling. I was lifted by their joy and naturalness.

The thought of death is more frightening when we don't talk or think about it. Three years ago I had to wait ten days for an operation to see if my breast cancer had spread to my lymph glands. Five days before the operation, fear hit like frozen air. I decided to let the fear just be there. It gripped me for most of the day, paralyzing me. Then I allowed myself the thought that I had tried to banish from my mind: "Well, I might die a whole lot sooner than I'd planned. I may have to give up my dream of being an eccentric old woman in a rocking chair looking at the Montana mountains. I might not see the world get better. I might not write another book." So I let myself be sad and afraid for several hours.

Then a lighter thought sprang into my mind: "I may die in my fifties but I probably won't die this week or even this year. I can probably finish another book, spend some time in Montana, and I'll probably feel a whole lot better if I get up to do the dishes." The fear slipped away. I got up and washed the dishes and enjoyed waking up to a clean kitchen the next morning. Whenever the fear started to return, I simply said to myself, "I may die. I don't want to die, but I'll live through it." Just acknowledging my fear of death eased my fear of death.

Paradoxically, one of the tasks of the dying is to help the people who are left behind. My beloved Grandma Charlotte Davis died at home with us when I was fourteen and she was eighty-one. She brought the same dignity and presence to her dying that she brought to her life. About three weeks before she died she said, "I want to go to bed now, and never get up." She had made it clear she did not want to go to the hospital. In her final weeks I would run up to her room every day after school to see how she was. One day she said, "Charlotte, would you read me some poems?" She had never asked me for anything, and I felt so honored and glad to be able to read to her as she had done to me a thousand times as a young child although I was choking down my tears. That simple gesture helped me with her death. In giving me a way to be there for her she brought grace to the final task of life, which is helping one's loved ones through the dying process. A few days later she slipped into a coma. The next evening when my family was in her room, she woke up for a few minutes and asked us to kiss her good-bye. She died that night. There was a sense of completeness about her death.

Denying death is like denying our vulnerability. Opening up to our feelings about death opens us up to life. We are more likely to savor something when we know we have a finite supply. If we realize we have only a little time here on earth, it can help us put our energy into things that matter—peace, love, and joy.

38. SIMPLIFY YOUR LIFE

So far we've been talking about clearing the mind and freeing the spirit to make room for joy. It's also important to lessen the clutter in your life so you save energy and have less to maintain or worry about. Every time you fish through a cluttered drawer looking for something, plow through a closet stuffed with clothes, or try five pens before you find one that writes, you are draining your energy. Think about it. If you got rid of all the stuff that doesn't work, all the stuff you don't need, and had your home organized so that if you reach for something it is there, how much time and frustration could you save?

It's wonderful being in an uncluttered place. It's natural for some people to stay uncluttered, although it's difficult for me. Recently, I tore into my house, cleared things up, and threw out excess junk. It was deliciously restful to see open spaces and cleared-off counters and tabletops. There was literally more breathing room in the house and more breathing room inside of me. But along with the peaceful feelings, I also felt a twinge of discomfort because I had stripped away a distraction that left me feeling vulnerable and sad—feelings people express when they lose weight.

We can also declutter our lives with fewer committee meetings, fewer obligations, fewer toys for children, fewer words, and simpler gatherings. I am a great advocate of potlucks because no one gets exhausted doing preparation. Recently, my roommate and I had invited a few friends for a potluck and the house definitely looked lived in, but it was the first warm spring day and the thought of cleaning paled in contrast to taking a hike in the mountains. "Well," she said, "it will be a come-as-*we-are* party." And no one cared or noticed. In fact it was probably better because instead of being frantic and frazzled we greeted our guests feeling happy and energized by our hike.

There is a spiritual aspect to letting go of belongings and simplifying one's life. We devote less time to physical possessions and more time to the spirit. When we are less constricted, that deep, quiet place inside of us where wisdom and joy reside has air to breathe and time to come alive.

39. RELEASE BLOCKED ENERGY

While there are times we move toward joy by taking charge of our thoughts, there are other times when we need to let go of our rational mind and allow our inner world to sing, dance, jump, yell, leap, howl, and stamp, to feel grief, sadness, joy, anger, and happiness. Every time we bury our emotions, we contribute to creating a stiff, rigid, stressed, or numb body. One way to access our inner world is with movement and sound. It's like stripping away your self-consciousness and control and allowing your inner world to speak.

Recently, I went to a voice workshop as part of a solstice celebration. It was called, "Sing Till the Song Sings You." I had a tight chest and sore throat when we started. As part of the workshop we stood in a circle in the woods and made any kind of sound we wanted to. We didn't really decide what sounds to make, but we listened inwardly and *allowed* sounds to come out. Much to my surprise, I was inclined to moan as if feeling some tremendous grief, Ohhhhhh. Nooooo. After a while, heavy raspy sounds came out of me, then bright, high sounds. At the end of thirty minutes my chest no longer felt tight and my throat was completely relaxed. It seemed amazing, yet it is not so surprising. Energy vibrations can clear out tension. Getting into your body and letting the sounds and motions take over can be scary—like losing control. But you actually gain control because you access more of your inner resources. When we use sound and motion, our unconscious is free to help us bypass the weary world of words. It's like letting a wise part of you speak. All you have to do is step aside.

40. BE MORE CAREFUL

Have you ever:

- Started painting with your good clothes on and got paint on your sleeve?
- Picked up a table to move it without removing a dish or a lamp that fell off and broke?
- Not bothered to back up material on your computer, and lost a day's work?
- Tried to screw the nozzle on a hose with the water running and got yourself all wet?
- Put some important records in a file folder but not labeled the file and spent hours looking for them?
- Put off phoning to find the date of a get-together and missed the party?

Get the point? This is the "stitch in time saves nine" part of moving toward joy. A couple of minutes for taking the time and energy to change clothes, put the dish away, back up your disks, turn off the faucet, label the file, or make a phone call can save you the frustration of ruining expensive clothes, sweeping up broken glass, or searching for important papers.

You might feel that you have to force yourself to leave what you are doing to go back and change clothes, get the right tool, or label a file, but it feels so good when you do, kind of like being a grown-up. And it leaves more time for sitting in the sun, or watching the rain, or simply feeling joy.

41. BE LESS CAREFUL

There are times to give up having your bases covered and take a plunge. You can write down all the pros and cons of making a decision, but at some point it's time to let go and do it. This doesn't mean you don't check things out when you buy a new house, take a new job, plan a vacation, or get into a relationship. It means at a certain point you stop being picky and worrying about every little thing and just do it. Yes, there may be flaws, it may not go perfectly, but it's folly to think you can prevent all difficulties.

Imperfect situations can be part of the fun if you see them as drama. Living richly in the spirit involves risk and pushing through fear. So immerse yourself, plunge. Go with your joy, your dreams, your love, your life. Live in the middle of your passion and your heart's desire. Jump in the sand, visit your old friends, take the rafting trip, change jobs, join a choir, tell someone you care about them, buy that little house. In short, expand. Don't be imprisoned by fears that constrict your energy and your joy.

For some people, expansiveness comes easily. For others, it's like walking through terror—an immediate "But what if . . . " screams in their head. They think of all the things that could go wrong instead of all the things that could go right. I suggest that the next time you ponder a decision, *think of everything that could go right* and say to yourself, What do I have to lose, really??!

MARVEL AT YOUR AMAZING BODY

42. REMEMBER THE MIRACLE OF YOUR BODY

We have been given a miraculous body to live in. Many religions and spiritual philosophies have made a separation between body and spirit. At worst people have been told to beat on their lowly flesh because it was of the devil. I believe our body is a blessing of creation, a wondrous home intertwined with our spirit, something to enjoy and care for. When our body is well and alive, it is easier to feel our spirit and experience joy.

So ponder your amazing body. Your brain can store vast amounts of information. Your heart has been pumping blood every minute of every day of your life, and your liver works day and night to detoxify all the toxins or junk food that get into your body. Your immune system, which works to clear out anything that doesn't belong in the body, has about a hundred million trillion molecules or antibodies, and in the time it took you to read the last two sentences your body has produced a million billion new antibody molecules. Just imagine! And now it has done it again.

When you run, talk, walk, see, move, a million billion things are working together in your body, like an information system more vast and intricately interwoven than all the phone lines in the world. Intelligence literally circulates throughout your body. If you injure yourself, your body immediately responds to the situation with adrenaline, blood movement, heart rate change, and so on. I remember going into shock one time and within seconds my heart rate dropped to 54, my temperature to 94. It was my body's amazing instantaneous survival response to a sudden trauma.

To help you ponder this marvelous body you live in, I suggest you watch the video *The Incredible Human Machine*, produced by National Geographic. It's available at many video stores, and it's one of the best deals for 99 cents I've found in a long time. Although the body is much more than the video title suggests, the show is inspiring, and inspiriting.

43. LISTEN TO YOUR HEART, ALWAYS BEATING FOR YOU

One of the first sounds you ever heard was the beating of your mother's heart. Like it was an echo in a cave, you heard it beating, beating, beating as you developed in her womb.

When you were only a few months old—womb time—your own heart started beating. And, unless you have suffered a heart attack, it has never stopped. No matter whether you've been happy, angry, lonely, sad, tired, joyful, or just muddling through every minute of every day, your heart has been working, like a loyal friend, carrying blood through your body, transporting oxygen and other nutrients, keeping you alive. At a heart rate of 70, it will beat over one hundred thousand times today!

Find your pulse. Listen to the beat. Imagine your heart sending blood, flowing out into your body, renewing you. The Sanskrit word for *heart* is *Anahata*. You might say it out loud: *Ana-*

hata. Anahata. Hear the rhythm as you say it. It sounds a lot like your heart, always beating, never stopping.

As you listen to your pulse, think of your heart as more than a muscle that pumps blood. There is an exquisite link between your heart, your brain, and every cell in your body—a constant feedback loop. The cells of your heart have intelligence similar to the brain. They respond to signals that you are being loved, cared for, and experiencing happiness. That's why there are endearing terms such as *sweetheart, honey,* and *sugar* for people we love. Loved ones nourish our heart. Love is sweet. Part of our journey toward joy involves nurturing our heart with love so we can hear the calling of our heart.

Anodea Judith writes in *Wheels of Life:*

We listen for the beat and fly, deep unto its sound.
We reach for ground, slowing down;
We still ourselves to listen deeper, quiet is the sound.

Deep within each person find the heart.
Everywhere around you find the heart.
Deep within ourselves we find the heart.
Every time we touch, we touch the heart.

44. COME HOME TO YOUR BREATHING

Breathing is directly related to joy, and conscious-breathing exercises are often considered the cornerstone of the spiritual journey. If you are feeling good, or you are feeling afraid, tired, sad, or lonely and disconnected from your spirit, you can come home to yourself by tuning into your breathing. Take a deep breath all the way down into your belly. (It might help to imagine a big balloon gently expanding inside.) Savor the fullness of the breath, then let it go, releasing *all* the air slowly. Do this a few times, then stay aware of your natural breathing for a few minutes. Follow it going in and going out. Some people visualize their breathing as a golden column of energy; others visualize a cleansing breath coming in and toxic or tired air coming out. Still others just breathe deeply without an image. Sometimes a sound, image, or word will help you go deeper. I say *Om,* or, *drop down,* or *let go* or *it's all right,* or *I am one with all,* or a phrase I was given by a meditation teacher. Sometimes I have an image of slipping into a starry night. These phrases or images help me release my thoughts, relinquish control, and sink inside. You can experiment until you find what works for you.

A deep breath is like a gift to every cell in your body. It helps your circulatory system, your brain, and your muscles. Deep, conscious breathing can slow the heart beat, lessen anxiety, lower blood pressure, help the body burn up toxins, trigger the release of endorphins, and assist us on the path to consciousness and joy. (Not to mention that it feels good and is free.)

Taking a few minutes in the morning to sit and focus on your breathing—in and out, in and out—will help center your day and bring greater radiance to colors and sounds. The difference may be subtle, but if you do it regularly and then miss a few days, you will notice the difference. As you sit and breathe consciously, your mind might wander. If it does, just bring your focus back to your breathing—in and out, in and out. This is the core of meditation: Be present to your breath, and when you slip away, come back. When we take time for conscious breathing, and slip between our thoughts, we are able to sink deeper and deeper down into an inner world both peaceful and vast. In this quiet place we become directly linked with our Knowing place that is at once within us and around us.

When I start my late afternoon empowerment spirituality group, many people arrive from work hurried, hungry, tired, frustrated, or anxious. We start the group with breathing exercises: first deep down in the belly to release tension, then in the chest to open the lungs and heart, then up to the tip of the nose, sniffing like a puppy. We bring our consciousness to our heads. After that, we make big yawning noises, do belly laughs, or get up and move around. All of this takes about ten minutes, and usually everyone is wide awake and present afterward.

There are many ways to energize our breathing—exercising, walking, playing tennis, meditating, practicing yoga, kundalini breathing—and they all help open our consciousness and literally nourish every aspect of our being. It's also helpful to notice your breathing when you talk with someone. Remember to let go of your breath as you speak, and if you are wondering about what to say, just take a deep breath, release it gently, and wait for the words to come.

Conscious breathing is also great for controlling your appetite. When I spent time at a spiritual retreat, I did conscious breathing and yoga before lunch. I would walk away feeling both full and light, as if I had eaten a cloud. Even though there was gourmet food, I ate lightly because I felt energized and peaceful.

So when you think of having that midmorning doughnut, lighting up that cigarette, or drinking the next cup of coffee, consider deep breathing instead. Sit quietly, or get up, walk, sing, get your energy moving. It's cheap, nonfattening, better for you, and there's no hangover or energy drop an hour later. You may feel resistance at first because eating a doughnut is easier and more familiar. But the path to joy takes a thousand small steps—like choosing between a doughnut and breath of fresh air. (By the way, if you do eat the doughnut, relax and savor every bite and be nice to yourself—it matters but it's not serious.)

45. USE YOUR INCREDIBLE MEMORY FOR PLEASURE

Even if you regularly lose your keys, forget where you parked your car, or misplace important papers, your memory stores more information than all the libraries in the world. Your brain is far more sophisticated than any computer. You may have forgotten an incident, and then twenty years later something cues that memory—a smell, a sound, a person, a picture—and instantly your mind recalls massive details about an event. Think of how many voices you recognize on the telephone. One time, a friend whom I hadn't talked to in twenty years called me. All he said was "Hello," and before he said his name I knew who it was.

A pianist pulls out a piece she hasn't played in twenty years, and while the first time through feels like wandering through a maze, within a few days she can once again play the piece beautifully. Someone starts reciting a nursery rhyme or a story you knew as a child, and it all comes back.

Another way to marvel at your amazing memory is to pull out old photos. As you look at them, notice how images burst upon your conscious mind. You remember a dinner conversation at Thanksgiving from thirty years ago; you can almost smell the turkey or hear your relatives arguing over what time to eat.

Another way to experience your wonderful memory is to reminisce with people about past times. Before I moved from Minnesota, one of the most healing ways to ease the separation of my therapy groups was to talk about turning points, the ways people had been helpful to each other, the times someone had been mad or wanted to leave. Often someone would say, Oh, I had forgotten that. We ended up laughing, crying, and appreciating the richness of our experience together—as if everyone had brought an ingredient for a cake and we put it all together. And somehow, with all the memories more alive in our minds, it was easier to part because we knew the memories would stay with us.

Sadly for some, opening up the memory bank brings back images of things like someone throwing the Thanksgiving turkey across the table, being pushed in the river at a picnic, being sent to your room for not eating your oatmeal, being given the cold shoulder when you said you were a lesbian. This kind of history can make the road to joy more arduous, but usually it is better to know than to repress our pain. One of the mystical gifts of human nature is that after we release the painful memories and express our grief and rage, we will usually be able to remember some good times and appreciate something about our families. Then we can move toward creating a community of kindred spirits who care for us, listen to us, and support our journey. Even if we have painful memories to work through, along the way we can use our amazing mind to create images and visions that bring pleasure and hope.

46. PLAY WITH YOUR IMAGINATION

I was once caring for some children who got into playful fantasies about their bodies. They imagined how long their fingernails would get if they were never cut or never broke, or how long their hair would be if it were never cut. Imagine your body replacing a pint of blood in twelve hours if you lose or donate your blood. Think about the millions of times today the pupil in your eye has gotten bigger and smaller, as you go from light to dark places. Figure out why the hair on your arms grows a certain length and then stops. How does it know to do that? Imagine that one million billion things are going on right inside of you this very minute . . . because they are. Imagine that with every thought you create new cells and change your body. And as you imagine the wonder of your body, think about loving your body, being nice to it, and appreciating deeply what happens when we walk, talk, see, smell, sleep, think, jump, twist, hear, feel, yell, throw a ball, hit with a hammer, sing, write, or read.

REACHING OUT, BREAKING THE RULES

Tips for Making Life Easier

47. IF YOU FEEL LIKE A BABY, GET A BABY-SITTER

Do you ever feel overwhelmed at the thought of doing a seemingly simple task? Do you ever get a strong desire to crawl under a blanket, take a walk, go to the store, eat chocolate, call a friend, or clean out a drawer instead of doing the task at hand? If so, you have a lot of company—including me.

At some point in my late forties (hopefully you won't have to wait so long), I decided to accept myself just the way I am, including the fact that I sometimes get anxious at the prospect of paying bills, balancing a checkbook, filling out insurance and tax forms, getting the leaves raked, setting out flowers in the spring, and getting organized to go on a trip, particularly when I have to do a workshop. Sometimes I start getting my notes together and thinking about what to wear and then I can't seem to stay focused on one task. I get scattered, and then a force starts rolling in like the tide, overwhelming me to the point where I fear I will run out of energy and won't be able to get everything done. My throat and chest tighten up and I feel like a little kid wanting to scream, "Mommy, help me. I'm too little to do this." Sometimes, at this point, I just sit down and feel paralyzed, or I run to the store for butterscotch drops.

In contemplating how to handle this anxiety, I asked myself how I could accept myself just the way I am and get through things like this. "Well, let's see. I feel like a baby . . . so maybe I need a baby-sitter."

The first time I let myself get a baby-sitter was when I made a quick dash to a New Age health shop to pick up some tincture I wanted to take on an impending trip. I was already feeling the grip of the anxiety and the loss of energy taking over. My bed was strewn with clothes because I couldn't figure out what to pack, and I was overwhelmed with an urge to crawl into bed and sleep. At the store I started chatting with a friend, Allanda, who has the most soothing, gentle energy of anyone I've ever met. I asked her what I could do for my anxiety. While we were talking, I blurted out, "Could you come over and help me? I feel as if I'm about to fall apart." She looked at me and to my amazement said she was off at 4:00 P.M. and would be glad to help for about an hour and a half.

When she arrived I felt like a distraught little child who was about to be picked up and cradled in a mother's arms. Just having Allanda sit with me in my room and pick up one article of clothing at a time and say, "Want to take it? Or should I hang it up?" helped release the tight grip in my throat and chest. We went into the kitchen and she helped me do the dishes, which had also become an overwhelming task.

I have deduced that the part of me who had to be too independent too soon and who decided never to show her tears pays a visit when I am faced with a difficult task. It's as if a three-year-old is being told to fix dinner and do the dishes. But figuring out where it comes from doesn't always take the anxiety away.

Once I owned up to my anxiety, I started asking others if they got frozen or anxious trying to do various tasks. I spoke to a man who could scale mountains but had a terrible time grading student papers at the end of a semester. There was a brilliant physicist who got nervous trying to make spaghetti. And a professor of political science had anxiety attacks trying to balance her checkbook. In other words, it's not about brains.

I pondered this for a long time and thought back to my parents, particularly my mother, who never seemed to get as anxious as I do. I thought of her growing up with five brothers and a sister and having numerous relatives all living within a few blocks. Everyone helped everyone else, and no one had to be good at everything. When I was a child, my father fixed everything around the house, my mother sewed and cooked, and all four of us children had chores. Mother would take us out to every kind of orchard and farm to pick fruit and vegetables, which we would bring home and can. It was definitely a team effort, and one was seldom alone. Now we are often faced with running a household alone and have expectations that we should be able to do everything. In reality, most people have some tasks that reduce them to feeling about four years old.

Irene, a rehabilitation counselor, was chronically late getting her client reports written up. Every day, she gagged on guilt, seeing the file folders accumulate, and she worried about it on the weekend. Yet she felt powerless to get at them unless a crisis occurred—either her boss got mad or she needed the notes for court. We tried several tactics to get her motivated, but nothing worked. I suggested she get help. She kept saying, "I don't need help, I know how to do it, I just have to get started." She would also add, "I feel so stupid about this, I don't know why I'm such a baby."

I laughed and asked, "Do you want to know what I do when I feel like a baby?"

"Sure," she said.

"I get a baby-sitter."

She laughed. "But isn't that giving up?"

"Giving up *what?*" I laughed.

"Well . . . working it through?"

"Well, that's a nice idea," I said. "But what's life for? To be grueling it out all the time? When I get anxious trying to get ready for a workshop, I call my neighbor to come be with me. I get help organizing my writing."

"What kind of help would I get?" she asked.

"Hire someone to come sit with you and talk you through it, develop a new system—whatever you need," I said.

Irene countered, "But that costs money."

I laughed. "And these therapy sessions don't?"

She smiled, paused, then said, "So you don't think I'm a baby?"

"I think you are a normal, grown-up woman who sometimes gets overwhelmed. I think most of us have times when we feel like a kid wanting a mommy to help us."

So Irene hired someone to come in and help her get a system together. Then she asked friends to keep her company on Saturday mornings while she wrote her notes. Her Catholic guilt dogged her for a little while (things shouldn't be this easy, there should be more struggle) but she certainly felt a lot happier having her work under control.

So remember to ask friends for help sometimes. It is also wonderful if partners and loved ones can be "baby-sitters" for each other on some of these occasions—not as caretakers but as friends in need. It's much easier to do things when we're not alone.

48. IF IT'S WORTH DOING, IT'S WORTH DOING BADLY

Many people block themselves from undertaking new endeavors—from learning a language to taking up a sport or music lessons—because

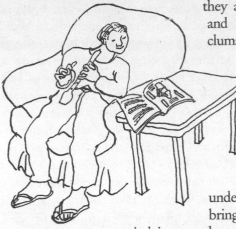

they are afraid of being clumsy and mediocre. I suggest that clumsy and mediocre can be wonderful compared with burying one's dreams and shrinking one's life. It is excellent for the spirit to be a beginner at something. Being a beginner keeps us humble, helps us understand children, and can bring tremendous pleasure if we stop judging ourselves and just enjoy. Better to be a run-of-the-mill piano player than go to the grave regretting you never tried.

My tennis game is a prime example. I'm definitely only an average player, but I'm proud of it. As a child I loved watching the ball bouncing back and forth on a beautiful spring day making a *bop* sound when it hit the racket. But I thought of tennis as a rich-kids sport or for people who were naturally gifted. I hungered to be one of them. One time I took my father's ancient tennis racket, with its huge grip, to play with a boy at school who said he would help me. I swung the racket and hit myself in the face, breaking my glasses and cutting my eye. I was terribly embarrassed. I tried again eight years later when a date took me to the unfamiliar territory of a country club to teach me tennis. I couldn't concentrate once I realized my tan shorts went against country club etiquette of wearing white. I tried again in my late thirties when I saw a notice for a summer recreation class. This time I stuck with it and even got into a league. Over a ten-year period, through many of life's dramas, I moved up four league levels (and down one, when I started writing books).

When you let yourself do something badly you don't have to

get caught up advancing or pressuring yourself. When I started having numerous tennis injuries, a chiropractor suggested I take a hot bath before playing and sign up for yoga. My only goal was to stop having injuries. But at the yoga class there was pressure to practice and to move up to higher levels. I said to the teacher, "I am coming here to enjoy the class, I have no desire to move beyond the introductory level, and I don't plan to make it a steady discipline. I will pay attention and do my best, but I don't want any pressure." I took the introductory class four times, started practicing a bit at home, and have never had a tennis injury since.

So consider doing what you always wanted to do—take piano lessons, learn to fish, try woodworking, take a class in Spanish, try aerobics, join a hiking club, plant a garden, take up golf. Whether you do it well, do it so-so, or do it badly, let yourself experience the magic of knowing that when you practice something regularly, you will always improve, and you will send messages of happiness throughout your whole body.

49. IF IT'S WORTH DOING, IT'S WORTH DOING WELL

While there are times to be happy with a mediocre job, there is something wonderful about staying with a project until it is absolutely the best you can do. Creating beautiful woodwork, precise stitchery, a beautiful painting, or a poem, or practicing something until it is all yours—natural, flowing, refined—gives a wonderful feeling. It can take hundreds of thousands of times practicing a tennis stroke, or playing a certain phrase of music, but when you get it, Ah! It's another form of orgasm or bliss— you feel alive, connected, at one with the muses.

Having discipline in one area of your life is a wonderful way to help you move toward joy. Going over something one more time, and one more time, and one more time helps bring all the

tiny details together into a perfect whole. When we stretch our mind, expand our capacity, we start to believe that anything is possible.

50. STAY AWAKE, STAY AWARE— LEARN FROM YOUR STRUGGLES

Sometimes we resolve to control a behavior and then find ourselves doing it again. At 8 A.M. we say we aren't going to eat sugar and at 10 A.M. we're munching on a sweet roll. We tell ourselves we shouldn't spend more money and three hours later we're ordering a new dress from a catalogue. It feels like something driving us that we can't control, but it's usually a substitute for a deeper, underlying need. Lonely? Eat. Angry? Seduce someone. Ashamed of a mistake? Blame someone.

The stay-awake-stay-aware approach helps you gain insight

when you are going against your principles but can't seem to stop yourself. The basic principle is that by adding awareness to a compulsive or addictive behavior you transform the behavior.

For example, Nancy says to herself with great resolve, "I'm not going to go out with Jack again. Never. He lies, he's mean, He's no good for me."

Then Jack calls, turning on the sweet talk. Nancy's resolve slithers away and there she is saying, "Hi, Jack. Yeah, I'm fine. Oh. That's okay. No, I'm not mad. Sure I'd like to get together. Yeah, you could come over here, I could cook you something. Oh, no, it's no problem."

After she hangs up the phone, she is devastated. "I've done it again. Four years of therapy, three years in Al Anon, six workshops, and seventeen self-help books, and I just invited him over for dinner. How could I do such a stupid thing!! I'm a hopeless case. Bad Bad Bad."

With the stay-awake-stay-aware approach, instead of launching into "What's the matter with me?" Nancy can observe herself. So as she shops for Jack's dinner, cancels a date with a woman friend, and cooks when she'd rather read a book, she asks, "What do I really hope to get from seeing Jack? Do I think he makes me more important? Am I trying to escape my loneliness? Am I afraid if I let go of Jack there will never be another? Do I want to be able to tell my friends I'm with a man?"

When Jack comes over, she can watch her own behavior. Does she suddenly feel and act like a little girl? Does she have sex when she doesn't really want to because she thinks it means he loves her?

After Jack leaves she can ask herself: Did I get what I truly wanted? If not, what are positive ways I can get the love, excitement, and comfort I want? Could I get comfort by telling a friend I'm lonely? Could I get companionship by asking a friend to go to a movie? Could I stay home and give myself a massage rather than having sex I don't want?

With the stay-awake-stay-aware approach you go through

your dramas with your self-esteem perfectly intact. You break the trance of the addictive behavior by attempting to tune into your inner world.

Teaching this technique has not always resulted in immediate gratitude from clients. I remember a woman who had been in numerous addictive sexual relationships bursting out at me, saying, "I just hate you. I hate you. I pick up a man and am about to have sex and then I hear your voice saying 'Stay awake, stay aware.' Then I can't do it. You're spoiling all the fun." This is the paradox of stay awake, stay aware: Consciousness and addiction cannot co-exist.

So instead of beating yourself up because you can't seem to give up a behavior overnight, be gentle, lighten up, and stay awake, stay aware. Slowly, as you observe yourself, you will start gaining insight and the addictive trance will lose its grip.

51. IF YOU'RE PLANNING A BINGE, INVITE A FRIEND

One of the barriers to joy is feeling ashamed of a behavior that is out of control. Inviting a friend to be present when you binge takes the stay-awake-stay-aware approach and adds a friend. This breaks the cycle of secrecy and shame. You ask an understanding friend to come along just to listen to you saying out loud what is happening when you binge. The friend is not there to give you advice, but rather to listen and possibly ask a few questions or make an observation at the end.

If you are out of control and ashamed of eating, shopping, or other compulsions, invite a friend along on a binge. This can be done in two ways: First, if you are slipping into a binge, call a friend and ask them to be with you. (It's a good idea to talk this over in advance and have the friend agree to be a support for you.) The other way is to simply plan a binge and do it consciously, having a friend with you so you can reach inside and talk about what is going on with you. In either case you use the stay-awake-stay-aware approach and talk through everything that is going on in your head.

One time when I suggested to a woman in a group that she invite someone over for a food binge, she looked at me quizically. "You can't have a friend with you on a binge!"

"Why not?" I asked.

"Well . . ." She laughed. "You have to do it in secret—otherwise—uh, well, that would take the fun out of it."

"And the shame out of it?" someone else remarked.

"Well . . . yes."

Another woman joined in. "Yeah. Shame is part of the high. You get to binge and then say what a horrible, terrible person you are."

Being with a friend and talking through a binge can be very powerful. The very act of saying things out loud— "I'm eating this whole pie because my mother was critical of me on the phone yesterday" "I'm buying this blouse because I'm lonely"—starts to crack through the unconscious game. It often seems quite funny. As you say, "Here I am, punishing myself by eating a pie because my mother was critical" you realize it doesn't

make much sense. You begin thinking, "Just because my mother's critical of me doesn't mean I have to satiate myself with pie."

This approach involves transformation rather than quitting something cold turkey without understanding. It's a form of healing from the inside out by not making the addictive behavior the enemy. This enables you to let go of your addictive or compulsive behavior gradually from a point of compassion and understanding and create a deeper bond with a friend.

52. IF SOMEONE'S THROWING GARBAGE OUT THE WINDOW, MOVE

Knowing when to stay in a situation and when to run is part of the dance of joy. I learned the throwing-garbage-out the-window metaphor from a psychologist. I had felt that some friends were putting unreasonable expectations on me to take care of their children. I had tried explaining my stance and we had had a couple of phone conversations, but their expectations remained unchanged and their anger increased. I was confused about what to do or whether I should call them again.

After considering the situation, my psychologist said to me, "I think you've done quite enough. If you were standing under a window and someone was throwing garbage out, what would you do?"

"Move," I said.

"Right," he said. "You can't stop garbage from falling out the window, but you can sure step out of the way."

If a Mack truck is coming down the road at you, run. If someone is falling-down drunk, get out of the way. If the house is burning, get out.

Knowing when to move can be life saving. My father once told me of a trick question he used in a college class on forest fire control. If there was a fire coming from a certain direction and wind was coming from another, what was the best thing to do? The right answer was, "Run like hell and pray for rain," but few students ever got it. So allow yourself the freedom of knowing there are times to bail out, quit, run, leave the struggle, and have more time for joy.

53. SET YOUR GOALS, BUT KEEP YOUR EYE ON THE PRESENT

It's fine to make goals for your life, to have a plan. It's especially important for women who don't often set long-term goals because they don't take themselves seriously or assume they will be taken care of. But the dance of the journey to joy involves being open to detours in the road. For example, if your goal was to get a college education, but after a couple of years your heart is longing to work in Alaska, then don't be imprisoned by the goals, let them go.

I got married thinking I would be married all my life; after four years of depression, I left the marriage. I thought I would be a piano instructor in a university the rest of my life; then I had a clear calling to become a psychologist. I thought I would be a psychologist the rest of my life; then I started giving workshops and have become an

author. Now I don't plan the rest of my life. I try to listen to my calling and follow the guidance that comes to me. The idea is to live by the truth, not a plan hatched twenty years ago.

To stay tuned to your path requires that your mind remain focused on the present, which provides a constant feedback loop that helps you assess and reassess your goals. We pick up signals in our mind, body, and spirit that tell us if we are doing what is right and true for us. This can be related to work, friendships, or leisure time. If you start hating what you're doing or who you're with, get depressed, have lots of aches and pains, drink a lot, have a chronic knot in the gut, engage in constant rationalizations—maybe you need to reassess your path and relationships. Many times, we love something or someone for a while but then a time comes when we're through learning from that person or situation, and it's time to move on.

One of the mysteries of life is how our path unfolds. And joy in life comes from the way we either accept or fight our path. Listening to our hearts and our bodies and tuning into the things that bring joy is core to the journey.

WHEN YOU'RE SINKING,
GRAB A LIFE LINE

54. FIRST AID FOR HARD TIMES

On the path toward joy we sometimes meet with intense pain and depression. Sometimes a person is simply trying to get through a day and just cope. This section is offered as first aid for those times. And if things are tough for you right now, hang in there! People care, I care. Many people have moved beyond depression and despair—including me.

Breathe. Sit down, tune into your body, and follow your breath going in and out, in and out. If your mind jumps around, just keep coming back to your breath. Stay with it.

Say, "I am sacred no matter what." Whether you're depressed, rageful, scattered, or falling apart, remember—it is just a part of life's dance. At your core you are still a sacred person, worthy of dignity and respect, especially from yourself.

Say, "It matters, but it's not serious." It's a drag and a pain in the neck to be depressed, anxious, or upset, but it means nothing about your worth. The point is not to shame yourself for feeling badly, for that will only make you feel worse. You can say to yourself, "I'm simply feeling scattered or depressed [or whatever]. It's not bad. I'm not bad. It happens."

Tell yourself it will pass. When we're sinking, we tend to forget that we've been through this before, and that we're likely to get better. You have skills to help yourself feel better. You can say something like, "Lots of people get scattered/depressed. They get over it. I can get over it, and there are probably techniques to help me I haven't found yet."

Put your attention outward. When you're sinking into a grim morass or feel like an overwhelmed child trying to figure out adult problems, let go of finding solutions or thinking of the past or future. Focus on concrete things around you: Count the ceiling tiles or the books on your shelf; notice the curtain rods, the door frames, the light fixtures; look at the details in a picture; get up and move around the room and, if possible, go outside and take a walk. Keep tuning into your breathing and count the trees near where you live. Do anything to get your focus outside yourself. The problems will wait. Don't try to solve them until you feel more centered or grown up.

Play music. Sometimes you might play upbeat music and other times you might play something that helps the tears flow. Think of whatever comforts, delights, or touches you. Listening to music can help keep you from feeling alone because it brings a connection with sound, words, music, and other people. It's like bringing light energy into a dense situation.

55. TAKE CONTROL OF SOMETHING . . . ANYTHING

Usually when people feel anxious, get scattered, or lose control, they are feeling overwhelmed. There are too many demands, and the self feels too little or inadequate to handle them. (This is also true in dreams where you are being attacked or assaulted and feel powerless.) The goal is to recognize that you feel overwhelmed, accept yourself, and then take steps to regain control. Say that you are going to do something and then do it without getting sidetracked.

Here is an example of getting scattered a friend described to me: I start upstairs to get a book and stop to wash the bathroom sink. I go to turn off the bedroom light and then start trying on old clothes to see if I should give them away. I then start to do the dishes and stop to make a phone call. I want to write a letter and start cleaning out my desk. It's as if a voice of distraction hops into my mind, keeping me from following through with my intentions. After a couple of hours of this, my stomach churns, I feel like crying, and I want to crawl into bed to escape feeling so out of control.

One way to gain control is to make a simple list of things to do. It doesn't matter what's on the list, so long as the tasks are easy. *The point is to chart your course, follow it, and don't give in to the voice of distraction.* A list might read: Sleep for one hour. Hang up my coat. Walk around the block. Wash five dishes. Call a friend. Do five minutes of yoga.

You can talk yourself through it like a loving parent would for a small child. "I will set my timer and take a rest. Now I will get up. I will now hang up my coat." When the voice of distraction says, "Oh, hey, look at the magazine," ignore it, and keep saying, "I am going to hang up my coat. I am now hanging up my coat. My coat is hung up. Ah! Next. I will now wash five dishes. (Oh wouldn't it be nice to call Deb.) I am washing five dishes. Five dishes are now washed. No I won't wash ten or clean out the silverware drawer. Next. I will put on my coat and walk around the block. I am now walking to the closet. I am putting on my coat. I am walking out the door."

As you take control, you may feel a part of you rebelling and trying to distract you or make you sleepy, but if you hang in there long enough, you are likely to feel the anxiety slipping away. Once you have mastered these simple tasks, which will help reinforce your sense of confidence, you can start thinking of other things you need to do to take charge of your life in general.

If this doesn't work, sleep and try again. You probably need a rest and a break. You may also need to talk yourself through your fears or call for a "baby-sitter." In any case, be nice to yourself. The last thing you need is someone shaming you and putting you down—especially you. That's probably what got you so overwhelmed in the first place.

56. CONNECT, CONNECT, CONNECT

We have talked about feeling overwhelmed or feeling like a child. Usually when children are upset they need to get rest, be held, be reassured. There are several types of connections that can help us out of an emotional jam. We usually need to do one or more of the following:

1) Connect with feelings.
2) Connect with another person.
3) Connect with our spirit.

Connect with feelings. When you suddenly feel disconnected, scattered, self-abusive, or nasty to others, it can be the result of repressing feelings about an event that recently occurred in your life. Backtrack to when you first got off course. Did you not stand up for yourself when you were angry with someone? Did you feel misunderstood and not tell anyone? Have you been rationalizing your feelings and need to be honest with yourself?

Once you connect with the event that preceded getting off course, ask yourself what you wish you had said, how you felt about the situation. Then, after getting clear, ask yourself the question, "What can I do about it?" You might need to talk to a friend, talk to the person who hurt you, talk with a therapist, yell, or say one hundred times, "It's not my fault she acted that way." Even if you never plan to talk with the person you're upset about, you can let yourself know what you feel and what you would like to say to them.

Connect with another person. When we're in a crisis or being hard on ourselves, making a connection with another person can reassure us. No, we're not unlovable to the core. No, we're not the only one who ever blew it. Yes, other people care about us even when we get scared or make mistakes. Talking with another person can bring back perspective on our situation. The goblins in our mind get bigger in isolation, just as a child left alone in a dark room can't get over thinking there is a monster in the closet until we turn on the light and take a look.

If you tend to tell yourself you *shouldn't* bother people with your troubles or that you *should* figure it out on your own, you may have to push through shame to call someone. But on the path toward joy, connecting honestly with another person and sharing your vulnerability is crucial.

To prepare for these situations, you might at some point make a list of names of friends you can call and put it by the phone. Many people forget they have a friend in the world when they start feeling lost or ashamed. To make it easier for yourself, you can also check with a few friends to see if it's okay to call them when you're upset. (Also have them agree that if they are busy they will be honest and tell you so. That way, you won't pick up inattentiveness, which is hard to take when you're down.)

Connect with your spirit. Simply remember, this is drama, it's not about your worth. You are sacred, you are life. You have the capacity for joy no matter how buried it seems at the moment.

57. WHAT TO DO IF YOU *STOP*

Lots of people tell me one version or another of stopping. It can happen either suddenly or after a time of feeling frustrated and out of control. But suddenly, that's it, you can't think or concentrate anymore and you want to sit in a chair and stare in space. Milder versions of stopping are what I describe as slowdowns, like when you're trying to clean up the kitchen and it seems to take forever. You just can't seem to mobilize yourself to finish.

Here are some things you can do:

Make peace with your stopping. I say to myself, "Hmm. That's interesting. I'm stopped. It's okay to be stopped. I may get stopped periodically the rest of my life, but I can manage it. Lots of people get stopped. I will get unstopped. I always do."

Do something comforting. For me, the best thing to do is take a short nap (that's what overtired children need) or make a pot of relaxing herb tea and just sit in a comfy chair and breathe deeply and look out the window. Sometimes a brief walk helps. Most of all it's important to quit pushing yourself.

Don't shame yourself or put yourself down in any way. Putting yourself down is like spanking a child who is overwhelmed. Elicit your kindest, wisest self to help you through and then talk to your friends about it. Remember that lots of successful, terrific people, stop.

Think of something pleasurable to do. If you keep trying to force yourself to do the task at hand, you will probably get more frustrated. But it may help you to think of something completely pleasurable. Many people get stuck because they continue to shame themselves and try to force themselves to get going. When your body and spirit stop, they're telling you something. Listen. When we fight ourselves, we clash inside. When we follow the signals our body gives us, we start creating trust in our inner wisdom.

58. SAY "HELP" TO THE UNIVERSE

Many people find it helps to say (or think) "Help" when they are afraid, upset, befuddled, confused, scared, or overwhelmed. Like a great big yell to the universe "Help" calls forth powers around and within. "Help me find strength. Give me energy. Give me courage. Help me through. Guide me. Be with me." Call it prayer, call it what you like, but by saying "Help" and acknowledging our distress, we open ourselves to the vast powers of the universe as well as our own wisdom. And if we don't believe there is power outside of us to listen, one very important person will have heard the call—you.

59. REMEMBER, YOU GET TO MAKE MISTAKES

Part of finding joy is in accepting ourselves when we make mistakes. Many people start sinking into despair or scolding themselves unmercifully after making a mistake. It seems like a crime to break a glass, forget a meeting, mail an important document to the wrong address, or spill coffee on a letter. *The important thing to remember is that everyone makes mistakes—me, you, everyone!*

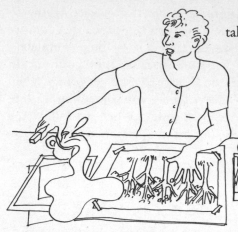

It's important to put mistakes in the context of life. Your mistake probably seems bigger to you than to anyone else. Generally, people get heated up over a mistake because they feel shame— they think there is something wrong with them if they make a mistake. Here's a list of things you might say to yourself to help you stay gentle and loving:

- All people make mistakes.
- It's natural to make mistakes.
- I can go back and apologize.
- I can probably clean up the mess.
- I'm not bad for making a mistake.
- It's just a small cosmic blink in time.
- In a week it will not matter, and even if it does, I'll survive.
- I can make mistakes and still be loved.

Then put the mistake in perspective. "No big deal." The earth will still turn, people will still have babies, the fish will still swim, and you will still be sacred. I find it a paradox in this culture that people who make decisions to drops bombs that kill and maim thousands of people give themselves less grief than someone who spills a glass of milk on the kitchen floor.

So ease up on yourself. Just because your parents screamed and yelled when you made mistakes doesn't mean you have to do the same.

60. DON'T SCRAMBLE YOUR EMOTIONS

When you are trying to get clear with your feelings about a situation, it helps to talk about one emotion at a time. Sometimes people start talking about their anger and before they finish, they interrupt themselves to talk about their sadness, or rationalize the situation with long explanations. As a result, no thought or feeling is ever played out completely, and they keep going in circles.

I was once in a workshop with the pioneering family therapist Virginia Satir. She helped me talk about my feelings about my father, who was dying of Alzheimer's disease. I started to express my sadness about my father, and then I quickly jumped to my anger. Virginia put her arm around me and said, "Do one emotion at a time. For now we are talking about your sadness. Put your anger in another place and we can talk about that separately, but don't mix up your emotions." I have remembered this wise teaching for years and it has been helpful in working with others.

If you are going to talk about your anger, talk about all the ways you are angry until you have expressed all your anger. Don't interrupt yourself, don't rationalize, don't make up reasons. If you are going to talk about your grief, talk about all aspects of your grief, your sorrow, your loss, your unhappiness. If you are going to express appreciation or gratitude, express it without throwing in some qualifying statement that dilutes it.

As you stay focused on one

thing, you may hear the voice of an internal censor. "You shouldn't be thinking that." "They'll go away if you get angry." "Don't get so emotional." "How can you be so ungrateful?"

It may be scary to stay with a feeling or thought, but constant self-interruptions keep you from joy because you don't get to the heart of your feelings or the heart of the situation. Getting deeply inside yourself creates a secure base from which to make decisions or find solutions.

Allowing yourself to stay focused on your own emotions will also help you be a better listener for others. People who interrupt their own flow of feelings often interrupt others as well or say things to stop them from feeling or expressing their truths.

How does this relate to joy? Jumping from one idea to another is based on fear of our inner world. It keeps us from intimacy with ourself and others. When we allow ourselves to go deeply inside, fear subsides and we are able to relax, be open to ourself and others and less likely to avoid situations that put us in touch with our feelings. Thus we expand our lives, create deeper intimacy, and feel more joy.

61. BLOW "I CAN'T" TO THE WINDS— YOU ALWAYS HAVE CHOICES

No matter how bad life seems or how powerless you feel, there are still choices you can make. It may be little choices, it may not be the choices you'd like, but they are choices. For example, if someone is hitting you, you can choose to say, "Why are they doing this to me? What's wrong with me? I'm no good." Or you can say, "This is painful, but I'm not a bad person. How can I get out of here?"

If you just got fired, you can make a choice. You can have a fit, be mad, continue complaining and seeing yourself as a victim, or . . . you can get mad and then start thinking of all the new possibilities. If your lover just left you, you can say, "I'll never find another person. I'll be alone. I'm no good." Or you can say, "I hate this, I'm mad, I'm sad, and I'll get over it."

It's crucial that you avoid saying "I can't" rather than thinking of the choices you do have. "I can't" throws up a road block in the mind and stops your creativity and flow of energy. I remember being irritated at my father for saying to me as a child, "*Can't never did anything*," but now that phrase dances in my head, a reminder that I always have a choice.

People who've had a lot of therapy (and some who haven't) often say they can't do things because of what their parents did. One time in a therapy group when a woman in her late forties said, "*I can't* talk back to anyone because my mother didn't let me do that," I leaned over to her, looked her in the eye as if about to say something profound, and said, "Get over it." The whole group cracked up because therapists aren't supposed to talk that way. I also said to her, "Is it going to be in your obituary: 'Died at ninety never having spoken up for herself because her mother hit her at five'?"

The point of remembering that you always have a choice is to keep you from being in a joyless victim stance. The world does hand us some tough times, but if we want to move toward joy we can say, "That was a nasty blow, it wasn't fair and I don't like it," and then make a choice about what we are going to do about it— hopefully a choice that will help us take action, improve our life, move on, and find joy.

LOVING YOUR BODY
IN SPITE OF IT ALL

62. IT'S HOW YOU FEEL,
NOT HOW YOU LOOK

You were given an amazing body. What is it like to live in your body? Do you think more about how your body looks than how it feels? If so, you are missing an important step to joy. It helps us move toward joy when we have abundant energy that flows throughout the day and our body feels strong and agile—like a good home to live in. No matter what your age and physical abilities, there are many things you can do to feel more alive in your body.

Sadly, in our culture we give far more attention to how our bodies look than to how they feel. What if we took all the time we spend on our looks and put it into creating a healthy, flexible body?

In Western medicine, health is often seen as nothing more than a lack of pathology—a lump, fever, sore throat, or illness. We aren't given many models of health as a person with abundant energy, who wakes up bright and clear. It is not necessary to forge the perfect body (which is only an illusion) or cultivate the right image to feel joy. I've had absolutely stunningly beautiful clients who were suicidal, had few friends, and had never enjoyed sex. Yet I've known ordinary-looking folks who pour forth the milk of human kindness, speak from their hearts, spread joy, and have long-term committed relationships and a satisfying sex life. Think about yourself as a spirit that lives in a physical body. Your true beauty comes from taking care of both your spirit and your physical body. This creates a glow of vitality, which is very attractive.

A huge step to joy is to say, "I accept my body just the way it is today." It doesn't mean you wouldn't prefer some change, it means that you accept your body right now. You may need to affirm yourself many thousands of times—we have been given a lot of negative programming about body image. My friend Linda told me that she refused to be weighed when she went to the doctor. I thought, what a great idea, and decided to do the same. So when the nurse points to the scales, I just say, "I'll pass on that," or, "I don't weigh myself." It feels great not to reduce myself to a number and then get upset because of that number.

When you start getting obsessed about your looks, age, or size, just tell yourself, "This is not the voice of love, joy, or my creator. I am sacred just as I am." I'm not saying it's wrong to look nice or want to lose weight, but if you equate your looks with your intrinsic lovability, you are walking away from your spirit. It can be fun to wear pretty clothes and look good, but when it comes to clothes you might ask, "What would I *enjoy* wearing? What is *comfortable* for me?" not "Can I seduce someone by wearing this? Will someone approve of me if I wear this?"

Imagine a world where beauty is equated with people who radiate vitality, warmth, peacefulness, and joy. Imagine accepting yourself and others just as they are physically, seeing through the surface to hearts and souls. Such a perspective could change how we live and love and bring us all closer to joy.

63. EXERCISE, EXERCISE, EXERCISE (OR, OXYGEN, OXYGEN, OXYGEN)

A crucial step to living happily in your body involves exercise. Exercise increases your flow of oxygen, which is good for your immune system, your muscles, and every cell in your body. Exercise and oxygen help you think more clearly, feel more peaceful, and have more energy. Exercise stimulates the endorphins in your brain, which brings feelings of pleasure (endorphins are also stimulated by sex and chocolate). The more pleasure we get naturally, the less we will reach for counterfeit pleasures.

I wish all schools would include stretching, breathing, folk

dancing, and eurythmics as part of the daily curriculum and instill the belief that exercise is just as important as food. Eurythmics involves moving, walking, clapping with different rhythms and beats, which helps coordination and brain integration. Children are also taught to express themselves through movement. At the deepest level the rhythms and music become internalized in the child like a pulse beat, completely natural and integrated. This lays the foundation for feeling deeply in tune with the body and for musical studies. Instead of counting the beats, you feel the rhythm from the inside. If we incorporated these basic developmental skills, health problems would decline and children's self-esteem would rise because they would feel better, perform better both physically and mentally, and have more psychological resilience. It would also help us reach adulthood with an exercise habit.

If you didn't exercise as a child or are out of shape right now, you can start today. Five minutes a day is better than none, and after a while you'll want to do more because it feels so good. You can do mini exercises all through the day that include deep breathing. Better yet, set aside a chunk of time to stretch, breathe, sweat, limber up, take up a sport, walk, hike, run up the stairs, jump on a trampoline, and get moving.

If you are resistant, talk to that part of you: "I know it's hard, but it will get easier. I only have to do it a few minutes a day to start. I'll feel so much better in the long run." You can make bargains with yourself. I stick to my rule of going four times a week to the gym, but I let myself do exactly what I want. I see what hums for me—walking, swimming, stretching, Nordic Track, weights, whatever I want. That way, I don't build up a lot of resistance. And remember, the ego resists most at the beginning of change. So the main thing is, do it! Do it badly, do it awkwardly, do it anxiously, do it briefly, but just do it.

If you are limited in movement by age or disability, exercise the parts of you that you can move, and imagine exercising the rest. If your brain is engaged while you exercise, the results will usually be more profound. For example, if you are doing back exercises, keep your concentration on the place you want to heal or loosen up, and imagine it becoming strong, healthy, and agile. According to my physical therapist, focusing the mind can increase healing by 50 percent or more.

The incredible lesson from sustained exercise is realizing the power we have to make changes in our bodies. We can become stronger, more flexible, more agile, and improve our wind capacity in a few weeks. People of every age who exercise show marked slowing and even reversing of the aging process. And because the body and mind are interwoven, we also improve our mental capacity, clarity, and sense of well-being at the same time.

As an aside, we also need to remember not to become compulsive or driven about exercise because that can defeat the relaxing, healing benefits. While we may need to nudge ourselves, the point is to enjoy it, be in touch with our bodies, and internalize the realization that we have within us a tremendous capacity to affect our state of health and well-being. A woman I know expressed the wonder of healing from an injury by doing exercise. "It's like feeling close to God, just knowing that within me lies the power to heal my body and feel well again."

64. WAKE UP AND KNOW YOUR BODY

Part of finding joy involves getting in touch with our bodies and realizing we have the ability to give ourselves pleasure. A wonderful way to wake up in the morning is to massage yourself in some way. You can rub your abdomen in a circle, do pressure point massage on your arms or chest, rub up and down your arms with your hands or knuckles, use featherlike strokes, or do whatever helps you wake up and feel a sense of well-being.

Many of us were brought up to think that we get pleasure for our bodies only from other people. When we know we can give ourselves pleasure, we become less dependent on others.

Not only will self-massage bring you pleasure, it will also help you realize that you can play a role in healing or helping your body. Recently when I started to practice the piano after a long break, my index fingers were extremely sluggish. So along with practicing, I started pressing a line on my forearm that felt like an extension of my finger right up to my elbow. I would press at about one-inch intervals. At a couple of places I hit a tender spot so I stayed there for a while. Within a few days the dexterity in my index fingers improved dramatically.

When you massage or put gentle pressure on tense spots, it can result in a rosy red spot where the blood rushes in. You are opening up the energy in a blocked place. Once you start doing a morning wake-up for your body, let your instincts be your guide. From your head to your toes, get to know yourself—the loose parts, the tight parts. Many food co-ops and health food stores have little charts that list the pressure points in your hands and feet. Even without you knowing the exact points, you can just start pressing down your arms and legs, your skull and body, and find the places that are tight and the places that enjoy being touched.

Many people get uneasy when they think of giving themselves physical pleasure. But if our creator gave us a body so capable of pleasure, then to feel the wonder of our bodies is to connect with the magic of creation.

65. BECOME THE LOVER
WHO KNOWS YOU BEST

While there is no substitute for a warm embrace and sweet kisses, one's sex life need not stop just because one doesn't have a lover. And even if you do have a lover, part of finding joy involves staying connected to your body and remembering that you can also be a wonderful lover to yourself.

A friend once said to me, "Sometimes I make a date with myself for two hours. I clean up my room and take the phone off the hook. Then I start with a scented bath. I have soft music and flowers and I slowly, sensuously touch my body all over. I explore myself, thinking of what feels good. I try different touches. I might spend an hour in the bath, then I go to my bed and massage and love myself some more and then eventually stimulate myself to orgasm." She talked about the deep feeling of intimacy she experienced that had come to parallel the closeness she had felt with a beloved partner. This is scary for some people. They think they are being disloyal to a partner, that it is self-indulgent, a sin. Or perhaps it brings up painful memories. But I don't believe that loving the body that houses our spirit could possibly be a bad thing when done with tenderness and love.

Once you know what it is like to be loved in a way that includes your whole being, you can bring this awareness to your sexual relationship with a partner. Let your partner know how you like to be touched and don't allow anyone to touch you in a way that feels wrong or violating to you. On the path to joy, sexuality, love, and respect become intertwined.

66. YOU ARE HOW YOU EAT, HOW WILL YOU BE TODAY?

Your amazing body works best when it is fed healthful, natural foods. Our bodies are ecological systems just like the earth. Our moods, energy, and mental clarity are related to the foods we eat (as well as our genetic makeup). All systems in the body attempt to keep a balance. For example, we sweat, shiver, breathe, eat, drink, and eliminate to maintain a steady temperature of approximately 98.6°. It's quite amazing that we can go from external temperatures of +90° to −30° and yet our bodies maintain the same temperature. Likewise, the body is always trying to maintain a balance in

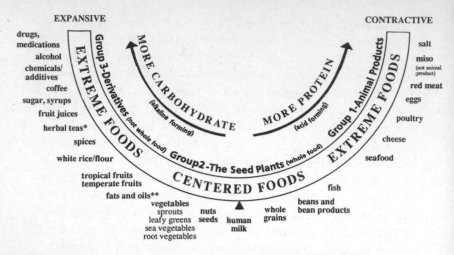

EXPANSIVE

CONTRACTIVE

MORE CARBOHYDRATE (alkaline forming)

MORE PROTEIN (acid forming)

Group 3-Derivatives (not whole food)

Group 2-The Seed Plants (whole food)

Group 1-Animal Products

EXTREME FOODS

EXTREME FOODS

CENTERED FOODS

drugs, medications
alcohol
chemicals/ additives
coffee
sugar, syrups
fruit juices
herbal teas*
spices
white rice/flour
tropical fruits
temperate fruits
fats and oils**

vegetables
sprouts
leafy greens
sea vegetables
root vegetables

nuts
seeds

human milk

whole grains

beans and bean products

fish

seafood

cheese

poultry

eggs

red meat

miso (not animal product)

salt

*In general herbal teas vary from yin to yang according to whether they are flower, leaf, seed, or root in that order.
**The effect of oils varies based on whether they are plant or animal derivatives, quality, and method of processing.
Overall, the effect of yin and yang varies based on quality, freshness of food, preparation, cooking time, seasoning, etc.

Adapted from a model by Sol Miller with Jo Anne Miller.   Placement of foods on the scale by Shelley McCoy, certified macrobiotic cook.

relationship to the foods we eat. Look at the accompanying chart. If we eat foods high on the expansive side—the yin side— we will crave foods on the contractive side—the yang side— because the body is trying to maintain balance. This can result in constant cravings throughout the day. Thoughts of wanting a Coke, a candy bar, a beer, or some chips keep interrupting our conversations with others or our attention to our work. If we eat balanced foods (from the middle of the chart) we will typically feel more grounded and have fewer cravings, which helps us stay present to the moment we are in.

We seem to understand that aspirin, caffeine, valium, and alcohol have an effect on the brain and the body, but we don't seem to realize that carrots, apples, and cabbage are medicine, too. We can choose to use good medicine or bad medicine. As Joan Matthews Larson, director of a recovery program for alcoholism and depression, says, "A physical substance in a physical body has a physical effect." Part of the journey toward joy is not to be controlled by cravings but rather to feel a peacefulness and balance with food.

A phrase I have found helpful comes from Judy Smith, who works with eating disorders. She writes, "You are *how* you eat. How will you be today?"

You are how you eat. How will you be today?

deprived	loved
abused	nourished
punished	cherished
neglected	respected

There are lots of other words you could add to the list.

Many parallels exist between our cultural consciousness about food and the ways we treat the earth. Think of the above words as applied to our relationship to the earth. To grow more food, we use artificial chemicals instead of natural fertilizers, and eventually we deplete and destroy the soil. We push our bodies to do more than is natural with the use of sugar, caffeine, nicotine, salt, heavy oils, steroids, and overprocessed foods. As a result our adrenal glands and immune system are compromised and we become chronically tired and sick, and lack clarity of thought.

The effects of what you eat may be subtle and you may not feel the results right away, but, like the earth being overloaded with toxins year after year (creating a hole in the ozone, acid rain, and polluted air), our bodies and immune system slowly feel the impact of toxic eating.

Food has a profound effect on every part of our being—physical, mental, and emotional. Changing our food habits also means changing our relationship to the signals of our bodies. Instead of responding to sleepiness or chronic exhaustion with caffeine, nicotine, salt, or other stimulants to keep us going, we could recognize these as signals of the need to slow down, take a break, get more exercise, or change our eating habits. *Imagine asking noth-*

ing more of your body than it can give you naturally without stimulants. In the tradition of Buddhism, "When you are sleepy, sleep. When you are hungry, eat. When you are full, stop."

Unfortunately research money is being spent to create pills that help us lose weight when we eat too much, rather than helping people learn to eat according to the needs of their bodies. There are many different approaches to eating. Mine is simple: Stay as close to the earth as possible. Use fresh, unprocessed organic grains, fruits, and vegetables, lightly cooked or raw. If you use meat, poultry, or fish, use only a little, and use organic. Avoid stimulants such as sugar, caffeine, and salt. Get tested for allergies. Find treats that are good for you—don't get rigid about your eating or deprive yourself. And then, listen to your body. Everyone has different rhythms and needs. Once you are used to feeling vibrant and alive you will immediately notice the connection between what you eat and how you feel.

67. LOVING FOODS THAT LOVE YOU BACK

Our criteria for choosing food is often taste. We often associate ice cream, steak, coffee, sweet rolls, cream sauces, chocolate, and alcohol with celebrations and joy. But if joy is about balance and harmony, a contradiction exists because these foods weigh us down and do not contribute to our health. When we go against our "survival mind"—our early programming about what brings comfort—we are likely to rebel. In other words, a binge will usually follow deprivation.

The solution is to reprogram our minds to *love foods that love us back.* Imagine desiring only foods that bring health, vitality, and clarity of mind and help you wake up refreshed, in a positive state. The first step is to convince ourselves that foods make a difference in how we feel. Start noticing how you feel after eating certain foods. Do you get sleepy? Do the foods drain your

energy? Do they create cravings? Do they make you feel heavy or keep you from sleeping soundly? Do you wake up groggy in the morning? All these things can be related to food.

The second step is to train your mind to pair healthful foods with energy, vitality, health, less sleep, and waking up with a clear mind. You can say things like: "I'll be happier when I eat well. I'll feel better when I don't eat sugar." If you are at a gathering or faced with foods that you might enjoy but that don't contribute to your well-being, keep telling yourself that there is something you want more—your health and well-being.

Some people also use aversion techniques. When you think of heavy, fatty foods, you can imagine the fat being on your hips and raising your cholesterol level; feeling heavy afterward; the food staying in your system for a long time getting putrified; feeling groggy in the morning; needing more sleep; and the stomach, liver, and kidneys struggling to process and digest and use the food.

Think of eating as part of your spiritual journey. Eating in harmony with the body is a way of loving yourself and bringing peace and balance into your life. I use the affirmation, "I can love myself by eating well," and sometimes, "I can love myself by not eating sugar."

The last thing to remember is to be gentle with yourself. Old habits die hard. You don't want to associate guilt with food; you want to associate wisdom and self-love with food. So keep adding good foods to your diet, be gentle with yourself about the not-so-good foods you eat, keep listening to the signals of your body, and feel the joy that comes as you become more peaceful with food.

68. FEEL THE EARTH BENEATH YOUR FEET

Most of us walk thousands of miles in a lifetime seldom tuning into our legs and feet—until they hurt. To create more joy, feel your connection with the earth. Start tuning into your walking. Notice your gait, the feeling of making contact with the surface you are on, and let your body drop down, let go. When I use the Nordic Track and say to my body, "Let go, drop down. Let go, drop down," the little meter that registers my speed increases. I don't feel as if I'm doing anything differently, except that I stop holding my pelvis and let my energy drop into my legs and feet.

To make a connection between yourself and the earth, wear comfortable shoes. As you stride, heel-to-toe, feel the sense of rocking in your body, and let your energy drop down into your legs, releasing any part of your body you are holding tightly. Imagine your legs swinging loosely, carrying you. Imagine that the earth is sending energy up into your feet, legs, pelvis, lungs, and heart, helping you move and feel alive. And breathe. Even if you live in a tenth-floor apartment, it will work. The idea is to make contact with your legs, help them feel energized, and drop the energy down into your body and right through to the earth. This brings balance, a sense of rootedness, and connection with that great source of peace and energy—the earth.

LOVING CHILDREN, DISCOVERING OURSELVES

69. FINDING JOY THROUGH CHILDREN

Pregnancy, birthing, parenting, and teaching were subjects that frequently came up in my interviews with people when I asked about joy. A dear friend, Michelle, wrote me on the birth of her first child:

Dear Charlotte,
I am in awe of life and all its power and mystery. There is so little I can articulate, yet my body has experienced a very deep and rich understanding of creation. My body produced another. In addition to Andrea, I experienced another miracle: Both of my parents were witness to her birth at my invitation. Andrea provided an opportunity for the most profound healing for us all. Neither of my parents had been present (or conscious) for a birth prior to this one. It was truly beautiful and liberating.

I have a dear friend, Ernie, who, after being widowed, remarried and started a second family. When asked about joy, he spoke of his son, Ben, who was five. "Right from the beginning I've been completely involved. It's totally different from the first round when I was away so much of the time. This time I'm part of everything and I'm learning how wonderful it is to be truly bonded to a child. Just looking in Ben's face, seeing him smile, and learning new things gives me joy." Ernie then talked about the ways his joy with Ben touched the rest of his life. "The creativity, fascination, and love permeate everything. You get totally immersed playing with a five-year-old and it helps you to be more creative in your research, and then it matters more to spend time with the people you love. It gets all rolled up into one big experience with many parts."

Not all the caregivers in the world are parents. Teachers, nurses, social workers, foster parents, neighbors, and counselors all play a role in nurturing children. Erin, a fun-loving, playful woman who taught fifth graders, said, "I love teaching. Children drag you up to their level whether you want them to or not. They keep alive the part of yourself that could easily die when you reach adulthood."

Tom, who stays home full-time with his two boys, said, "I've gotten in touch with a whole human side of myself. Being with children wakes up the feeling part of me that I had lost in being identified almost totally with my work. Since I've been home with kids I've learned about a different world—listening, being spontaneous, playing, and dealing with the immediate demands of children. It's always a balance between teaching some delayed gratification and not squelching their creativity and spontaneity." He laughed. "That's the good-day version."

"What's the bad-day version?" I asked.

He laughed again. "When I don't have patience, and lose it and yell and scream. I feel badly because of what they're doing and the way I'm acting. But I'm lucky, I have a great spouse and neighbors I can call and say, 'Help, I need a break.'"

Like many of the ways to find joy, being around children stirs up all our feelings. It is challenging and humbling, yet in the end it has a profound ability to teach us about ourselves.

70. LET CHILDREN BRING YOU BACK TO LOVE

Children cry. They are stubborn, demanding, difficult. They take away our freedom. Or is it us, the parents, teachers, and caretakers, who are stubborn, demanding, difficult, and take away the freedom of children? Caring for children is a dance between setting appropriate limits as caretakers and avoiding unnecessary power struggles that result in unhappiness. We can ask ourselves, "What if *I* didn't fuss over the messy bedroom, the spilled milk, or the toys in the living room? What if *I* didn't start a power struggle over food, clothes, or bedtime?"

If a toddler reaches for the dials on the stereo, do we see him as a troublemaker, say no, and give him a smack, which results in wails and shame? Or do we tune into the child's world—the fascination and thrill of a new discovery? We can say, "Oh you like those dials," gently remove the child and say, "Those are for big people but here are some toy dials you can play with."

The hard times with children challenge our ability to love. One mom said, "Sometimes I have to reach for the love to pull me through. When she is crying and fussing, or being difficult, I start to get angry and frustrated, but then, because I love her so much and want her to be happy, I get creative in figuring out what to do. The love helps me let go of my anger at having my peace interrupted."

When we bring willingness to know ourselves and grapple with our feelings, we will grow and the children will flourish. A friend who has a two-year-old daughter said, "I never felt that I could draw or paint. In painting with my daughter, I just started doing it as part of playing, and all of a sudden something broke free inside. The part of me that is always watching and criticizing my artistic abilities went away and I became a mom having fun with my daughter."

71. PARENT THE NEXT GENERATION

Whether or not you have children yourself, you are a parent to the next generation. If we can only stop thinking of children as individual property and think of them as the next generation, then we can realize we all have a role to play. One of the crucial steps to joy is realizing that we are all connected and that when children around the globe are happy and cared for, we will feel happier ourselves.

So when you think about children, think of them as *all our* children, the ones who will carry our legacy. Consider ways you can support them growing up to be happy, productive adults. Offer an evening of care for the child of a single parent, over-worked parents, any parents. Include children when you have friends over, or volunteer to pay for a baby-sitter. Vote for school levies even though you don't have children or yours are grown. Volunteer at a child care center or a children's hospital ward. Find whatever avenue feels right for you, without wearing your-self out.

If you don't have much energy to give, maybe you could take a child to a movie or invite the parents on a picnic where you pre-pare the food. Even a phone call to ask, "How are you?" can be reassuring to parents. Too often we think of having to "put in our time" with children as if it were a chore or interruption from our lives. Remember that when we help care for children, we will probably receive as much as we give because they remind us of our capacity for spontaneity and wonder.

I spent a special time with a mother and child last winter. My friend Maryanne, and her daughter Jessica, nine months old, and I went for a winter hike and picnic on a remote ridge. Jessica was napping in Maryanne's backpack. The snow was deep as we trudged up the hill. "Isn't she beautiful?" Maryanne said to me, with the glow of a mother who is truly in love with her child. Later we sat under the pine trees on a plastic table cloth, eating oranges, crackers, and cheese. There was a panoramic view in three directions. The sun was warm and the snow was bright. Jessica came to life and played with an orange. We rolled it back and forth, then pulled out another toy for her so we could eat the orange. We laughed about taking food from a baby. A chill set in and we packed up to go. As we walked down the path, I saw Jessica alert and happy in her mother's pack, looking at me and smiling. I was overwhelmed with a sense of being present to something sacred that has existed throughout the ages—the bond between a mother and child. And within me I felt the stirring of joy, just being part of this circle of life.

72. WORRY LESS, HAVE MORE FUN

If I could summarize my suggestions to parents over the past twenty-five years it would be: worry less, criticize less, preach less, listen more, have more fun, be more honest with your own feelings, develop your own joys and friendships, and don't sweat the small stuff (which is nearly everything). The goal is not to be a perfect parent, because no such thing exists. The hope is to be a good enough parent so that your child leaves home a responsible adult who can take care of him or herself.

When you take a light perspective, it's easier to step back and relax when your child doesn't walk until fifteen months, is slow to cut with scissors, is not interested in playing ball, wants to be a cheerleader, doesn't want to be a cheerleader, has clothes strewn in the bedroom, has difficulty making friends, hates piano lessons, is awkward and shy, reads a book while you are driving through the Grand Canyon, gets caught shoplifting, flunks Spanish, has orange and purple hair, or is lesbian or gay.

One of the important things to learn about parenting is that *the more you worry about a child, the less the child will worry about him- or herself.* And, the more worried you get, the more the child will give you something to worry about because it makes the child feel powerful. Instead of worrying, watch with fascination and wonder as your child's life unfolds, and help the child take responsibility for his or her own life.

A technique I learned from Foster Cline, a child psychiatrist who works with attachment and bonding, is the Good Luck response. It helps keep parents lighthearted—it takes worry away from a parent and puts it in the child's lap, where it belongs. For example: When a child is coming home with endless blue slips because he or she is not turning in their homework, you can respond by saying, "Well, gee, you're getting a lot of blue slips. This will be a new experience for me. I've never had a child repeat the seventh grade before. Good luck with this." In other words, couch your response in a way that shows you as an interested but not a reactive adult. *The child gets to have the problem and doesn't have the power to destroy the adult.*

In another example, a teenager is running around with some questionable friends who tend to get in trouble. The parent can say, "Well, Randy, with those friends you are hanging out with, good luck," implying, "You're going to need it." When children can't upset parents with their behavior, it helps the children stop and think about what they are doing—which is what needs to happen. The best thing about the approach is that it is good for the child and much less stressful for the adult. So everyone wins.

73. GIVE THE GIFT OF HAPPY MEMORIES

The job of caregivers is to provide children with roots, then give them wings. A life-long blessing for children is to fill them with warm memories of times together. Happy memories become treasures in the heart to pull out on the tough days of adulthood. You can make lots of mistakes, but if you give children avenues for creativity and joy, they will have resources to carry them through. For example, if cooking together, reading, listening to music, coloring, participating in sports, or taking a walk in the woods are paired with pleasure and closeness, throughout life doing these things will kindle old feelings of happiness and/or comfort.

It's not so much that you *teach* children to do things right, but rather you help them associate pleasure with doing something. Set a good example and they will learn on their own. Then, if they show great talent in one direction and want to go for it, help them by getting good teachers and cheering for them.

My mother was a wonderful teacher when it came to cooking and sewing. I could feel how much she enjoyed being with me and my sister. It felt like some form of a mother–daughter ritual. As a teenager, I baked on Saturdays to have treats for weekday lunch boxes. My mother never criticized me, even when I used different food colorings in all the cupcakes, spilled all over the floor, or changed recipes—sometimes with disastrous results. I love cooking still and I'm good at it because it is relaxing, creative, and paired with warm memories.

It may comfort you to know that if your child reaches the age of eleven or twelve and you have a good bond or relationship, no matter how dramatic adolescence becomes, your children will probably turn out all right and want some form of connection to you in adulthood. So lighten up. Save the lecture. Remember, *It matters, but it's not serious.* Love matters. Self-confidence matters. It's all fleeting. Underneath the surface is a little person with big feelings, growing up, struggling, scared, tender, brave, desperately wanting your unconditional love and approval. Give it. It is the greatest treasure on earth.

74. LITTLE PEOPLE HAVE BIG EMOTIONS

It's a tough job to be little and to maintain a sense of dignity when adults treat you like a cute object. If we can think of children as having emotions just as adults do, we might change our behavior toward them. My rule of thumb is, don't do something to a child you wouldn't like done to yourself—like having a stranger walk up to you and tap you on the head, tweak your arm or cheek, say "Isn't she cute," and then laugh when you cry or try to pull away, and say, "Oh, isn't she shy."

Most people don't laugh when a friend is afraid, upset, or crying, but people do it routinely with children. Imagine that your car got smashed up, you were feeling lousy, you broke down crying with frustration, and a friend started to laugh. You would feel horrible. Children feel equally upset when a toy breaks, someone goes away, or they have been shamed. They need understanding, not adults thinking that little people's tears and frustrations are cute or something to laugh at.

So when you meet a young child or a baby, just be there and tune into their body language. If you reach out to touch them and they pull back, look annoyed, or turn their head, take it as a signal to back off. And in general, don't stare, tweak them, pull on them, or tap their heads. Usually children will come to you when they feel safe.

How does respecting children connect to joy? For the child, it fosters a sense of self-respect. For the adult, it helps tune into others in a more sensitive way. It can lead to greater sensitivity and understanding in all our relationships, including the child within us.

75. EMPATHIZE WITH CHILDREN: IMAGINE BEING WITH GIANTS

Imagine standing by someone three times your height—that's probably someone fifteen to twenty feet tall. Now pretend you are totally dependent on this person to feed you, love you, hold you, and protect you. This is the world of childhood.

Imagine this huge person shaking a finger in your face, shouting at you, "Bad. Stupid! Can't you get it right!" Or crying and pleading with you, "How can you hurt me like this? You're so unkind. You'll be the death of me yet." When parents scream, scold, and point the harsh finger of blame, it is overwhelming to the child. When a parent gives a child the message that they have the power to destroy them, it is guilt producing and gives the child a distorted belief in their own power.

Now imagine the giant person smiling down on you, showing delight or reaching down, scooping you up, holding you, rocking you, and looking at you with adoration. Imagine the giant on bended knees, coming down to your level, looking you in the eye, and being with you.

Now take these images of the giant and bring them into your adult relationships. When someone loves you, you may seem like a giant to them and your unkind words can cut like a knife. Likewise, your thoughtfulness, warm words, and respect provide great comfort and warmth. Then go one step further and remember that you probably have a giant part and a child part within you. So listen to yourself. Are you talking to yourself with kindness and understanding? The more you do, the more you will live in harmony with yourself and move toward joy.

76. NOURISH THE INVISIBLE BOND

To experience joy, a child needs to feel safe. In the womb, a child is bonded to its mother by an umbilical cord, the source of food and life. After birth, the child needs a *sense* of an umbilical cord to feel safe. It's like a comfort zone. Early on, a child can venture three feet away and feel safe so long as the mother or father is near. Like going to a feeding station, the child returns to the parent for a moment of reassurance and connection and then ventures out a little farther and explores for longer periods of time.

It is crucial that parents and caregivers be aware of the invisible bond children need to feel safe. When children go beyond the invisible bond, they are likely to get scared and cry. This is especially true in strange, crowded places (imagine what it feels like to be looking up at a lot of fast-moving giants). What they usually need is a hug, a touch, some warm words, a friendly glance, or someone simply moving closer to them.

I watched a toddler on the beach sitting beside a bucket, a shovel, and a stick, crying and fussing while his mother read about fifteen feet away. It was clear that the child didn't feel safe. He was whimpering and whining and the mother scolded him for being so much trouble. But when she picked up her chair and moved within six feet of him, you could see his relief. He stopped fussing and began playing quietly and happily while she read. She had cast a safety zone around him. He could feel the invisible bond.

In another instance, I was sitting in a doctor's waiting room watching a tiny child in a stroller, maybe nine months old, who desperately pulled at her mother's leg. It seemed obvious that she was reaching for a connection so she could feel safe. Unfortunately, the mother, who was reading, snapped at her, "Stop that!" and the tiny child started to wail. Then the mother got mad. Initially, all the mother needed to do was reach down, touch the child, look at her lovingly as if to say, "I'm here, we're connected, you're safe." If she had done that, she probably could have kept on reading and the child would have stopped crying and felt safe.

So remember, if children reach out, reach back, hold them, talk to them, validate the bond so they can feel reassured of their safety and protection in the world. Notice their body language. If you sense fear or panic, pick them up or get down to their level and be there and give them the safety they need.

As children grow older, they need the bond expressed in different ways. They are expressing the bond when they imitate you or want to join you in cleaning, walking, shopping. Recently on a canoe trip I enjoyed watching Mariya, a four-year-old girl, proudly carry her little paddle to the canoe and imitate her mother, Jeanette, paddling on the river. With older children, you can keep the bond by leaving notes after school, setting down the phone to smile and wave good-bye, or taking time to listen to the tales of woe from school or about the excitement over a new partner or the birth of a child.

It's not just for children that we bond. It brings joy to the adult as well, for there is little so precious as a human bond. I believe the world will change for the better as men start taking a more primary role in caring for children. It's humanizing, and it will help build common ground between men and women.

77. THROW AWAY SCRIPTS

Many parents have scripts written for their children when they are born. My daughter will not play with Barbie dolls. My son will excel in sports. My child will love reading. My child will wear cute clothes. My kids will go to college. My daughter will be a doctor. My son will go fishing with me. My child will take over the family business. My children will get married and supply me with grandchildren. It's one thing to have hopes, but if you have a script written for your children's lives—no matter what their age—burn it as fast as possible and send the ashes flying to the wind. Then look at your child, really look, and ask with all your heart, Who is this person? What is her nature? What is his heart's delight? How can I support this child finding *his* way, developing *her* talents, living through *her* disappointments?

Children know somewhere deep inside that you have a script. They will either go along with your script (and kill off a part of themselves) or defy you (and not get to find themselves because they will be so busy opposing you). My mother had a script for me. She wanted me to wear pretty clothes, be popular, join a sorority, marry a lawyer or doctor, and have grandkids for her. I was afraid as a child, clothes never seemed to fit right, I didn't make friends easily, I spent many hours a day playing the piano, I had no interest in sororities, I was a political activist, I hung out with bohemians and liberals in college, I got divorced young, and I focused on my career. In other words, I was a big disappointment, and I carried that knowledge like a wound in my heart (supporting a lot of therapists) until I finally realized it was *her* inability to love me. It was *her* loss. It occurred to me that I was a wonderful daughter whom any mother would have been proud of.

Think of having a child as scattering a packet of mixed flower seeds on the ground. You don't know what will pop up. It could be bachelor buttons, daisies, blue bells, lilies, poppies, marigolds, or sunflowers. You know it would be futile to yell at the poppy, "Be a daisy!" or tell the blue bell she should be more like the lily. So carry this analogy to your view of children (and friends). Say, "The reality is, my child is like this. That's just the way she is. My task, my challenge, is to love and accept *this* child just the way she is and enjoy watching and supporting *her* journey as it unfolds."

One way to learn about yourself from this is to check out whether your desire for your child to do something or be a certain way is your desire for yourself. Maybe *you* want to take piano lessons, *you* want join a softball team, *you* are concerned about your eating habits, or *you* want to make more friends. If you do, it will be a wonderful way to parent your children because you will present a model of a growing, stretching person, living in the center of your own life.

78. BLESS CHILDREN WITH UNDERSTANDING

If a child is crying or is upset, he or she needs to be understood just as you and I need to be understood. You don't have to fix the problem, take it away, or make it better—you simply need to be right there with the child, connecting with the experience. You can get down to eye level with an upset child and say something that reflects your understanding of what the child is feeling, such as, "Oh, you're upset," "You're afraid," "You're scared of going to the dentist," "You don't like your teacher at school," "You hurt yourself," "You're angry," "Oh the dolly broke, you feel bad." Invariably, the child will look up at you, slow down the tears, nod his or her head, and say yes. Being totally present in this way is often all it takes to repair the hurt because the child feels understood. It's another form of reinforcing the bond between you.

Too often, in an effort to stop the crying or ease their own inner discomfort, parents make fix-it statements. "They didn't mean to hurt you" (implying that you shouldn't feel hurt or you should rationalize everyone else's behavior). "Oh, it's nothing" (implying that your feelings are too big). "You'll get over it" (implying that it's not okay to be upset right now). "You're just wonderful no matter what" (denying that the child feels lousy). "Here, eat this ice cream" (pairing comfort with food). "It's just a cheap doll, I'll buy you another one" (denying that the child likes that doll and feels upset this minute). "It doesn't matter if Johnny likes you" (denying that it matters a lot to your child that Johnny like him). Another approach people use to squelch the feeling of children is shame. "Big boys don't cry." "What's the big fuss about?" "You're so dramatic." "You're being a whiner." "You're so bossy."

I remember being with my nieces and a nephew at the funerals of both my parents. The children were so natural in talking about their feelings. I remember one of them saying, "I think we should put M&M's in grandma's casket because she loved them so much." So grandma was cremated with a large supply of M&M's. At the funeral of my father a few months later, I held one of the girls as we sat in a room with my father's casket. She asked, "Why aren't I as sad about grandpa dying as grandma?" And we talked about it. We talked about how he had not been himself for a long time, so in some ways it felt as if he'd already died.

So remember: listen, listen, listen, understand, understand, understand, and don't try to fix painful situations and stop emotions. This will also help us find joy because when we start listening to children and allow them their feelings, we listen better to become more aware of our own feelings and those of our friends.

79. LEARN TO SAY, "WHY NOT?"

In response to children wanting to explore, touch, or do something new, many parents have a knee-jerk reaction. "No, not now." "Watch out." "It's too messy." Try replacing these reactions with, *"Why not?"*

- *Why not* blow up the new balloons right now, in bed?
- *Why not* walk around the airport a little bit?
- *Why not* run around the store and look at things?
- *Why not* have a friend over tonight?

Think for a minute of what really could happen. You can always try giving children a bit more freedom and see how it works.

If a "no" or "not now" comes up because *you* are tired and *you* don't want the balloons left around, or *you* don't want to fix breakfast in the morning for extra people, then say the truth: "It's fine to blow up the balloons if you take them to your room when you are done." Or, "I can totally understand you wanting to blow up balloons right now, but I'm too tired to cope—but you can do it somewhere else." "You can have your friend over but you'll need to get breakfast yourself because I'm tired."

If you are going to say no, own it as your need. It's dishonest and confusing to imply you are saying no for the child's own good. "Oh, you don't *really* want to blow up the balloon." "I think you'd be happier tomorrow if you didn't have a friend over."

I recently saw a two-year-old in a waiting room at a tire store,

standing totally entranced, running her little fingers up and down the indentations in the tires—hardly a harmful thing to do. Yet her parents kept barking, "Don't touch that!" "Sit down." "Be still." And when she bobbed up and down on the chair—a totally normal thing to do—the father said sternly, "Do you want a spanking?" (Does any child *want* a spanking?) I kept thinking, What was wrong with her touching the tires? She was fascinated, quiet, enjoying herself, exploring.

In another scenario, I watched a family waiting for a plane, and the children were climbing up on a ledge to see the plane come in. The parents sat nearby, relaxed, smiling. The children were happy, fascinated, and talking with other people. The joy on their faces when the plane pulled in was infectious to all around them.

If you give your children some freedom to explore within reasonable bounds, it will be easier for you to have them around because they will be content and able to entertain themselves. If they can gently touch a few things on the shelf at a store, they will learn to be careful and not go ripping them off to rebel against your rigid rules. So remember, a child's life is one of exploration, fascination, and wonder. If you can join children in their world, you will immeasurably increase your ability to say, "Why not?" to yourself. And this will lead to more freedom, and more joy.

80. FOSTER CREATIVITY: IT'S A SHOVEL! IT'S AN AIRPLANE! IT'S AN EGGBEATER!

Fostering creative expression is a wonderful gift for children. A child with a fertile imagination who can get lost in playing, reading, and enjoying the outdoors has a valuable resource to carry through life. Along with being a source of joy, a fertile imagination and ability to play is like a sanctuary or an outlet for pressure. If a child is alone, rejected, hurt, or having difficulty, the ability to fantasize or work out feelings with play can make the difference between coping well and becoming a serious behavior problem.

Many years ago, I moved from one apartment to another in the same building with my newly adopted daughter, who was terrified of all forms of separations. She spent the whole day bathing her doll and painting pictures of big black splotches. We put the drawings in a book and called it "Moving Day." She was using her creative expression to deal with a difficult situation.

Allowing the creativity in children to flourish makes life easier for adults. When I was moving into my new house, my friend Tom came over with his two young boys, Owen and Walter, to help me unpack. To keep them occupied, we said they could play in the fireplace pit with all the couch pillows that lined a huge ring around the sunken area. We gave them blankets, stuffed animals, and dolls and let them have at it. They played for two hours building houses, hideouts, and heaven knows what. I remember thinking, "Those kids are sure good at playing." Not only was it a pleasure for them, we were free to unpack and enjoy each other.

Parents don't have to teach creativity to their children, they need to get out of their way and let it happen. Simply provide the raw material and your blessings. An example: I was sitting on a beach fifteen feet from a two-year-old boy who was playing with a bright-colored plastic toy eggbeater. He was happily using it as a shovel, then as a press to make designs, then burying it, then flying it through the air as an airplane, then trying to use it as an actual eggbeater. At this point, his mother looked up from behind a newspaper and snapped, "NO. It's supposed to be used like . . . " The child looked totally dejected and threw the egg-beater away. His creativity had become "wrong."

Raw materials for creativity are inexpensive and available. You can have a box with scraps of wood, nails, glue to play with. Old fabric, string, paper, stickers, scissors, and old catalogues are inexpensive and have lasting potential for fun. Goodwill shops and used-clothing stores are meccas for dress-up clothes or sandbox toys like old coffee pots and cookware. For less than the price of a few Barbie dolls, you can have a box full of costumes.

So smile when the children paint the cow purple and the dog green, spend two hours cutting up paper into chips, or wear two different-colored socks. Be glad they can play, and enjoy the show.

81. GET A GLOBE

One of my fondest memories from childhood is of looking at a globe with my father. "What's the biggest country?" he'd ask me and my sister. We'd spin the globe around and guess.

"Why don't people fall off?" I'd ask. Even with the explanation of gravity, I still couldn't grasp it. Then we'd talk about different people in the world.

"Does everyone go to Sunday school like us?"

"No," my father'd say. "There are lots of different religions in different parts of the world, and people believe different things."

I marveled that everyone in the world gets the same amount of sunshine in a year, although it's differently distributed. I couldn't quite understand how there got to be so many languages, and how they could be so different, but it gave me something to ponder. (I still do.) We'd talk about the different time zones and I'd picture people sleeping on the other side of the world while I was having breakfast. It was fun imagining that when we were having summer, while people in Australia were having winter. They might go to a beach on one of our Montana winter days, or have snow on my birthday in August!

The globe brought me a sense of wonder and adventure. I wanted to go to those other places and see how people did things differently. And, many years later, when I did visit other countries, I took my father's interest and fascination with me.

When we plant the seeds of fascination and respect for other people, we are teaching tolerance and peace. Children naturally accept others of different races or colors, and we can support the process. The broader our horizons, the greater our capacity for joy.

82. FIND CREATIVE WAYS TO COEXIST

Joy is best fostered when we assume there are win–win solutions for everyone in a household The more often that caregivers find creative solutions for coexistence, the better for everyone.

Beverly, a friend of mine, told me her family has a special hat they wear in the house as a Don't Talk signal. As for me, I'm a great advocate of earphones. It never occurred to me that I had to suffer through listening to loud music just because I had an adolescent. It never occurred to me I would have to stop playing the piano so my daughter could watch TV. It seemed fair that she could listen to her music. So we bought good earphones. My daughter could watch TV or listen to music while I played the piano or read a book. Sometimes I wore them, sometimes she did, sometimes we both did. Likewise, when traveling in the car, she had her own tape recorder with earphones. So I listened to flute concertos and she listened to current hits, and now and then we had a tape we both liked.

Many parents are caught between wanting to let their kids get absorbed in TV so they can have a break and hating the dazed look children get from being glued to a TV set. One way to practice peaceful coexistence is to provide children with tape-recorded stories. You can make them yourself or have friends read them from books you have. Children will become involved listening to stories the same way they get entranced watching TV, but it's better for them because listening to stories stimulates their imagination. Read a book onto a tape and give a child both the tape and the book. It's a wonderful gift. A child can learn to put a tape in a small tape recorder by the age of three or four. Also, children will be comforted by your voice in your absence and treasure the tapes for years to come.

So dig into your creativity and think of ways to coexist. It will make life easier for everyone and foster a happy, less stressful home. Children can create wonderful solutions when the issue is presented as a family concern. The question to ask is How does everyone win and get their needs met?

83. BE HONEST, BE NATURAL

Part of letting yourself experience joy around children is to let yourself be honest and natural. It's one thing to joke, play peek-a-boo, or talk baby talk with children on occasion, but, in general, you don't need a special tone of voice or way of talking to be around children. Just respect them as you would others and speak from your heart at a level that is appropriate for their age.

Children respond very favorably to people who are natural, unintrusive, and straightforward. Some people are uncomfortable with children because they think they have to know some special way to be, give them expensive presents, or enjoy playing with all their toys. The special way to be is to be your most natural self. If you really don't want to play a certain game with children, you can say so or offer an alternative: "I'd prefer to go outside and play with a ball."

I get particular pleasure helping children make stuffed animals or doll quilts or going to a park, so that's what I offer to do with them. If you want to set limits, do so in a kind, natural way. "The rules in this house are that you put away all the toys you take out. Is that a deal?" A wonderful world awaits you when you relate to children as little people. The love they will give you back is far better than gold.

(Actually, you can apply these solutions to all relationships—be natural, respectful, understanding and honest, and speak from your heart.)

84. LEAVE A LEGACY FOR YOUR CHILDREN

If you want to leave a legacy of comfort and joy for your children, pass on to them the stories of your life and your heritage. Alex Haley, an African American, was able to write *Roots*—an account of his ancestors' abduction into slavery and the subsequent generations that survived in the United States—because each generation was told to pass on the stories of their lives. Native Americans as well can return to the circle of their own spirituality and traditions because people secretly kept the traditional knowledge alive during long periods of terrible oppression.

Whether your children are little or grown, write down or tape record stories from your life—the traditions, your heritage, your beliefs. Include something about your feelings, thoughts, conflicts, joys, and heartaches as well. Your children may not be interested at the moment, but a time may come when they will want to know about *you,* the person, the child, the daughter, the son, the scared one, the brave one. And if you write most of it, put something on tape so they can have the remembrance of your voice. Your grandchildren will enjoy it as well.

Recently I came across a five-page account my mother had

written of her first two years of married life. A strong sense of her presence touched my heart as I read it. She recounted the times when my father was a district forest ranger north of Yellowstone Park and they rode on horseback throughout the area checking out forestry cabins. Those stories are a link back to her I would never have had if she hadn't written them down because she never told me about those times.

After my father died, I looked for a short article he had written many years earlier on his spiritual beliefs. I was entranced because it gave me a connection to his inner world that I had seldom known. It was a comfort and a blessing to have it, and I saw how much I had absorbed his spiritual values. The amazing coincidence was that my brother had also sought out the article and we both came to the funeral prepared to read the same excerpt.

We grow up thinking of our parents as *parents*. Then one day, we ask, Who are they? Sometimes we ask it after they are dead, and we live with the regret of never having known all sides of their lives. As I mentioned in an earlier chapter, one of the most profound aspects of parenting is helping children with the dying process. Whatever your history, it is part of your child's legacy, and by passing on the stories of your life you help your children connect with the circle of their heritage. It gives them strength, helps them understand themselves, eases the pain of saying goodbye, and brings them peace. And doing this may well give you a sense of completion and joy.

MORE YEARS, MORE WISDOM

85. OLD AGE ISN'T FOR SISSIES, BUT YOU CAN STILL FIND JOY

On a lovely Christmas eve gathering while visiting my parents in Connecticut, I met Emily. She was ninety-three, bright eyed, and easy to talk with. I asked her what it was like to be in her nineties.

"Well, it has been fascinating. It takes a lot of work just staying alive—getting up, feeding yourself, moving around . . . and I ache a lot." Then, she looked at me directly and smiled. "Old age isn't for sissies, I'll tell you . . . but I still have joy," she said. "I'm curious about what's happening in the world and I like to see my grandchildren."

Emily's wisdom about old age included making jokes about the creaks and groans of an old body, and creating a community of friends who help each other. While she didn't like being stiff and slow, she was clearly fascinated by inventing ways to manage daily tasks. She had become part of a network of people who shopped, cooked, and helped each other out. "Eleanor can still drive, so she shops for me. I can still cook so she eats at my house three nights a week because I don't mind cooking—if you call it that. It might be a pizza, or the same spaghetti thing three nights in a row with a slightly different flavor. Sometimes after dinner we go up and read to a cousin who lives upstairs and is going blind. I know there will be a time when I want to let go, but it hasn't come yet because I can still enjoy the flowers and being with my friends."

86. PREPARE EARLY

As you will see, this section on aging centers on interviews I did with several older people who have maintained their vitality and joy. The richness of their lives created more of a mosaic than a single thought of wisdom, so you will find several ideas included in each vignette.

I interviewed Pearl in a retirement home in Florida when I was reconnecting with an old friend, Kay, whom I had known as a child. When I saw Pearl coming into the dining room, I was struck by her beautiful carriage, elegant, sleek hairdo (chestnut brown), and blue, rust, and brown woven scarf she wore draped over her shoulder. Kay introduced us.

Shortly after we started talking, Pearl asked me if I knew about acupuncture. She was happy to have a receptive listener to share her excitement about her recent treatments. "It's been wonderful. Just a few acupuncture treatments helped loosen up my shoulder that's been hurting for years. I'm feeling better than I have in ages." She spoke of books she was reading on natural health. It was clear that this woman relished life and never stopped opening herself to new ways of thinking and new experiences. She invited us up to her apartment for a nightcap later on.

I was unprepared for the amazing decor in her apartment. "Yes," she said, sensing my reaction. "I always wanted a Louis XIV living room." I felt like a princess sitting there. She was most willing to be interviewed.

"What do you think is important to say to people about aging?" I asked.

"Prepare early," she said with solid conviction. "Find things you are passionate about, start young, and don't let your life get bogged down. Nothing automatically happens as you age. The people here who are interesting and fun have been that way a long time—you can tell it when they talk about their lives. They've had adventures, tried new things, read, and have lots of interests. When I talk about my acupuncture treatments they ask me questions and are interested. Others just look at me as if I'm strange and change the subject."

One of the developmental tasks of midlife is preparing for the years to come. It's important to reach inside and think of all that is exciting to you. And if nothing seems very exciting, then start experimenting to awaken the passion within. While we can make changes anytime in our lives, it is much easier if we start awakening our interests in our middle years (if not earlier) so that our lives keep moving forward and we stay passionate until we die.

87. MAKE PEACE WITH YOUR LIFE

Take what is given and make it over your way. My aim in life has always been to hold my own with whatever is going on. Not against, with.

Robert Frost

One of the tasks of aging is to make peace with your life and let go of regrets. When this task is done, we gain the freedom to explore our desires and live out whatever pleasures we have created for ourselves.

In thinking of older people to interview about joy, my former father-in-law, Lef, came immediately to mind. After drifting apart for many years, I decided to visit him in Florida. Widowed for over a year, he lived with his dog, Amber. He greeted me with the same graciousness and warmth I felt the first time I met him as his future daughter-in-law nearly thirty years earlier. I felt peaceful and happy in his gentle presence, and have since maintained the relationship because it brings me joy.

Lef has a remarkable capacity to "go with" whatever he is handed in life. Given his history, that is no small achievement. He lived through World War II in his homeland of Czechoslovakia, decided with his wife and children to leave with the clothes on their backs, go to a displaced persons' camp, and await resettlement in another country. After two years, he and his wife found work in the United States, eventually bought a home, raised their two children, and then retired to Florida. His wife had died from Alzheimer's disease the year before I saw him. I asked him his thoughts on joy. He paused, as if letting the thoughts rise to the surface.

"Joy to me is realizing there may not be that many days left. They should all be precious. I should not spoil them with things that are minor and unimportant. I try to find nice things which I enjoy, things I never had time for when I was working, like spending more time with my dog, reading, gardening, and taking walks."

I asked about his experience being widowed after so many years of marriage. "When you have time like I did, you are prepared for death. It's not like when you and your spouse are both in good health and suddenly without warning you are left alone. With Alzheimer's you are seeing the decline for years, and you realize that the person is somebody different than the one you knew all your life. I became the caretaker, and did all the meal planning and the housework and was with her all the time. So I was prepared.

"After her death I felt as if I was entering a new period of life. I was now alone. I had done what I could. I didn't have any remorse. I didn't feel any guilt. Going through this also gave me an acceptance that my days are coming. I don't know when, but I am not afraid of dying. The only thing I am afraid of is to be left an invalid. But most of the time I just keep thinking that I want to enjoy all the days that are left."

Unlike Emily and Pearl's lives, which involved close contact with many people, Lef's life is self-contained except for brief visits with acquaintances and a couple he visits twice a month. He is content with this arrangement. "I read, listen to music, I rent videos. I follow the public lives, and am interested in what is going on in the world. I also follow all the tennis tournaments. I used to play, not well, but I enjoyed it very much."

Lef had also made peace with his departure from Czechoslovakia. I asked how it had been. It seemed so hard to me, to imagine walking out of one's homeland. "Being forced to leave my country and move to the U.S. gave me a freedom which I had not had since I was twenty-four, because for all those years we were at war or occupied. We were not free and I was always afraid. I was afraid of people who may have been my friends because they could have been informing on me. This experience gave me a perspective on what is important—like being able to trust someone, enjoying your neighbors, and being free of fear."

88. STAY WILD AND KEEP YOUR SENSE OF HUMOR

Several years ago I looked up Kay Danmiller, a woman I had known when I was a teenager. I had been a baby-sitter for her children throughout my teens. I adored her. Initially I was intimidated by her corporate executive family whose credentials included Harvard and Wellesley, but from the beginning, she treated me as if I was totally special.

Kay was about 5'3", had wild red hair, and lacked all pretense. Most of all, she *connected* with people. When I came to baby-sit, she immediately started talking about real things with me—Was I

happy? What was important in my life? What were boys like these days? What was I writing about in school? Had I thought about where I'd go to college? And she was truly interested. One time I asked her what was the most important thing about living for her. She paused and thought for a while, "Being a *good* person—really *good* in all ways," and that phrase stuck in my mind.

Kay was the most spontaneous and playful adult I had ever met. She would go to corporate parties wearing funny T-shirts, colorful skirts, and low-heeled shoes when the style was little black sheath dresses and high heels. Her husband would often say, "Are you wearing *that*?" as she walked down the stairs, ready to leave. She just smiled and said "Yes." Sometimes she took me to a country club to baby-sit the children by the swimming pool. I got to charge all the hot dogs I wanted while she played golf. She acted as if I belonged there, although I had only seen country clubs in movies. Their house was a mess and the children were happy and fun to be with. They were creative and relaxed, and I never worried about damaging or breaking anything or doing something wrong.

Twenty-six years later, after a five-year search that included sending a heartfelt letter to the wrong Kay Danmiller, I found the real Kay living in a retirement home in Florida with her husband, Joe, who was recovering from a stroke. She greeted me as if I were the center of the Universe. I immediately felt the same way around her as I had as a teenager—loved, valued, and happy. The red hair was now gray, but she was still wild, exuberant, generous, glowing, full of ideas, relaxed, and extremely casual.

"I think I'm losing something up here," she said, pointing to her head, "but I don't care. The wonderful thing about losing your memory is all the exercise you get. Inefficiency is good for the muscles." She could reframe anything to make it all right. She loved being able to turn off her hearing aid to have some relief from the TV, a companion to her husband.

One of her children was going through a divorce and Kay made statements like, "It's fascinating to watch the changes they go through, and it's wonderful not to be invested in what happens. I just love both of them." And it was true. She was able to be a loving observer. "Besides," she said, "I really want to keep my attention focused on the novel I'm writing."

Alive, involved, passionate about writing, friendly, able to set limits and to reframe the troubles of aging so she could laugh instead of cry, Kay knew how to live, and she never stopped. She may have been aging in calendar years, but in spirit she was growing, creating, and bringing joy to those around her.

89. KEEP OPENING YOUR INNER WORLD

It is a sad commentary on aging that one in seven older persons in the United States takes Valium (according to Dr. Bernard Jensen, an authority on health and nutrition). This need for tranquilizers is possibly related to unresolved feeling, fears, hurts, grief, and resentments that create increasing inner pressure because they have been in captivity for so long. The need to be introspective and access the inner world never ends if we want to stay free as we age.

I remember my delight and surprise when Lyla's registration for a Reiki healing class passed over my desk. Although she is in her mid-eighties, Lyla is my "girlfriend." We laugh, we complain, we talk about politics, computers, natural healing, and writing (she's completed a novel about the time she spent in China). I can also call her if I need an understanding ear. One thing that had puzzled me over the years, however, was that while she was always responsive to phone calls and invitations and glad to be included, she rarely called me.

At the Reiki class, Lyla was an active member, asking questions and making humorous observations. People warmed to her immediately. Near the end of class, when we were talking about our experience, she said, "This has been good. I think I'm going to be able to make some important changes." She continued her explanation with the urging of the group. "I've always had a hard time inviting people to do things, yet I love to be invited. I know it's related to my childhood, because I always felt so much like an outsider. I've been realizing lately that I find myself more at home with people a generation younger, so instead of reaching out only to my agemates I need to reach out to my soulmates. It's still hard but something helped today. I have this feeling now I can do it."

Not only did Lyla stay active and alive on the outside, she was open to introspection about her childhood and continued to make changes in her life. There is no reason to believe that ability for introspection and capacity for change ever stops. I remember having therapy sessions with my parents when I was in my late thirties. One of the requests I made of my mother was to be more direct with me if she didn't like something I did. And she made a tremendous effort to do it. While the basics of our relationship never changed, the gift to me was that she tried. So often the problem is not that people don't care, it's that they don't know how, they lack skills. I have worked with many parents and their adult children, and have seen vast changes in relationships when there is effort and good will underneath, and the belief that change is possible.

90. PASS ON YOUR LOVE

As we move toward joy, our perceptions of people are increasingly grounded in the energy and spirit they radiate, rather than their status or physical appearance. There is great richness available to us from people who have walked before us. I write of older people in this book on joy not just to portray people who age wisely, but to remind people of all ages to look to our elders as both teachers and companions.

For nearly twenty years, my mother's cousin Margaret Wickes MacDonald was my friend, spiritual teacher, and the person who filled the gap left by a mother who had wanted a child cut from a different cloth. Simply put, Margaret loved me. In 1971, on a two-month camping trip to the West, I stopped to visit this barely remembered relative living in Missoula, Montana, whom I hadn't seen since I was nine. When I arrived, she emerged smiling from the picturesque, historic white house and embraced me with her arms and her love. I went back to visit her annually for the next eighteen years, until she died at the age of ninety, shortly before I moved to Missoula.

Frequently, when Margaret and I were sitting at her round oak dining table amid the junk mail and the wilting flowers, the subject drifted to death. She'd say things like, "The wonderful thing about funerals is that you get to see everyone," or, "My brother Tom is holding on until the family reunion, he won't die until afterwards." And she was right.

One time when she had mentioned several close friends who had died, I said, "How do you handle having so many friends dying. Isn't it terribly hard?" She raised herself up a bit, gave me a deep look that was both warm and commanding, and with the fullness of her presence said, *"Death is part of life."* Many people could mouth those words, but for her it was a reality. She had integrated the mystery of death into her life with a level of peace and acceptance I have only glimpses of. And I know in some inexplicable way that her comfort with death was directly related to her incredible passion for living.

Shortly after making a serious statement of this sort, she would lighten up. "But it doesn't mean I like losing all my friends," she went on. "I was complaining to my neighbor that most of my friends were dying, and she said, 'If all your friends are dying, you'd better get yourself some young friends.' So that's what I'm doing."

At another time, she talked about her husband's death some twenty years earlier. He had been seventeen years her senior and had been sick for some time. One morning he said he felt strange, and had been going in and out of a deep sleep, and Margaret asked him, "Well ... do you think you are dying?" He responded, "I don't know, I've never died before." And they laughed together on the last day of his life.

When my own mother died suddenly, Margaret was the first

one I thought to call. She listened to me and asked how everything was going and who was there. The content of our conversation was unremarkable, but as I write this I start to cry—because the memory of the comfort again sweeps over me. Her words were simply the medium through which she conveyed the love that permeated her presence. Shortly before the end of our conversation, she said, *"Now don't forget to laugh."* And that was such a help, because I was caught up thinking I had to be grim all the time because my mother had just died.

The next day when my sister Lenore and I went coffin shopping and were saying things like, "That lining is a bit too blah, mother wouldn't like it." "That one's too fussy." "Oh, here, Charlotte, look, this is a nice peachy one, don't you think it will go better with her skin?" "Yes, but maybe this rosy one would go better with her dress." Then suddenly we looked up at each other, recognizing the absurdity of the conversation, and broke out laughing together. And I knew it was all right to laugh because Margaret had said so.

Margaret had struck a balance between giving and receiving. She liked picnics and knew how to keep preparation simple. She would pull out a coupon for Burger King and say, "Let's go on a picnic. We can stop by and pick up the food." She enjoyed being with people and she had been of service all her life. At eighty-seven she tutored Asian children in English. She had been on many committees in her church, and only in her late eighties did she slow down her activities. Being with Margaret made me recognize the ability to separate an aging body from a growing spirit.

On August 19, 1989, I arrived in Missoula for a visit and went directly to Margaret's house, carrying my first book, which included an acknowledgment of her. I still remember seeing her sit down at the oak table, open up the book, and slide those arthritic fingers down the page until she came to her name. She looked at me seeming very pleased, smiled, and said warmly,

"Good. Good." Those were the words I had longed to hear from someone in my family. Afterward, we went out to lunch with my daughter and a couple of friends. When one of them asked Margaret whether she liked the food, she responded with her characteristic aplomb. "Well," she smiled, "do you want me to be polite or honest?"

"Honest," my friend Judy had said.

"Well, I was hungry so I ate it and it filled me up, but it was boring."

And that was Margaret to the core. The truth—simple, humorous, never cloaked in extraneous words.

I took her home, hugged her, and had my daughter take pictures of us on her back porch as we always did. I said good-bye and left for Glacier Park with my daughter.

"Now you'll come stay with me when you get back," she had said with an urgency that felt unusual.

"Yes," I had said.

That was the last time we ever talked.

She had a fatal stroke two days later. I got back to town in time to spend a quiet evening alone with her in the hospital. Although she was unable to speak and her eyes were closed, she made a gesture to me with her arm when I walked into her room. I held her hand and sat with her a long time. She died a few days later as I was driving back to Minneapolis.

Well, people said she died. To me, she never aged, she only lived, and in some fundamental way she is still alive because the legacy of her loving presence and magnificent spirit live within me and all the others whose lives she touched.

DANCING WITH LIFE

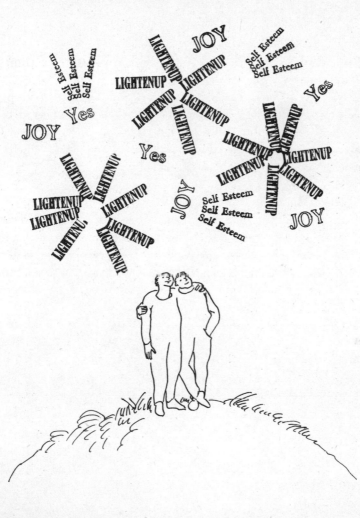

91. DON'T PATHOLOGIZE LIFE

Life is often messy, uncertain, and unpredictable. Sometimes it's a string of troubles that seem to never end. That's normal. Ups and downs are normal. Being ill on occasion is normal. Feeling peaceful and happy are normal. Occasional low-energy days are normal. According to Chinese medicine, it is accepted as natural that we fluctuate from being in balance to being out of balance. Peace of mind comes from not attaching a great deal of significance to either state. We simply note our moods and physical state and gently move toward balance as best we can, accepting it all as part of the flow of life.

We get ourselves into a corner when we believe we can avoid pain and problems if we only do it *right*—eat right, think right, pray right, image right, do spirituality right. Even with the best planning and organizing, we may have tough times or get sick, and even the "good" changes bring feelings of loss. The spiritual journey is not about getting rid of life's difficulties, it's about dancing with them. Life is not a sickness to overcome.

It's the nature of life that birthing, growing, loving, losing, learning, leaving, discovering, creating, dying, and being reborn stir up emotions. The recovery and New Age movements have sometimes pathologized life by considering every little feeling, problem, or headache as something to be figured out and overcome. Everything is given *deep meaning*. I call it recovery narcissism.

One response to being down or upset could be to simply do whatever brings feelings of comfort, security, and pleasure (without creating new problems like overeating or overspending). Another could be to ask the Universe, God, or Great Spirit to help you move toward a more peaceful state. Often chewing on a problem and talking about it over and over simply makes it worse. The answers are more likely to come when you are relaxed and receptive. You may wait a day, a week, or several months before the answers come, but in the meantime you'll be free to flow with life instead of creating more problems with intense worrying and pressuring yourself to get it all figured out. Wisdom has its own clock.

92. FOLLOW YOUR CALLING: LET THE STORY WRITE YOU

Many people want recipes for life—a list of rules to follow no matter what. Joy comes from spontaneity and going where the spirit leads us. The main guideline is to stay aware of the calling of your heart. Following our calling is not always easy, but if we ignore the wisdom of our hearts, we will feel split inside, and that's what leads to disharmony, addiction, and depression.

The path unfolds differently for everyone. Our task is to stay open, go where we are called, and not demand to know why. We may not understand why we are led to do something until years after we did it. Letting life flow is a bit like allowing a story to take its own form. You start writing with a plot in mind, but after the first chapter, a new character walks into your mind, and you depart from the original plan. You don't need to know why.

Surrendering to life means going where the energy is strong, where your body relaxes and your head stays clear. Usually when we go with the spirit we feel a sense of excitement or rightness, and that there will not be harmful consequences to you or anyone else. That doesn't mean it's easy or comfortable.

Joseph Campbell talked about following your bliss. I think it is more complex than that, because a calling does not always feel like bliss. A calling may feel clear and right, but it may also be challenging and scary. I remember feeling called to go to Athens, Ohio, which I loved. But then, after several years I realized I needed to leave to broaden my perspective. It seemed clear I should move to Minneapolis, although it did not fit my heart's desire for many reasons. It was there, however, I found healing for myself along with the resources I needed to finish my dissertation and write my first two books. It was right that I was there, even though it was never a home for my heart. It was also right that a time came to leave and go home to the mountains. Letting the story write us starts with *surrendering* to the messages from our hearts and *trusting* that following our path is truly the way to find peace and joy. This is the essence of living by our truths.

93. ORGANIC IS MORE THAN A WORD FOR FOOD

As the power of joy expands within us, we shift from wanting the biggest and best to wanting what is natural and organic. For example, a person decides to grow a prize flower: she plants the seed; gives it water, sunlight, and lots of chemicals to make it the biggest. She ends up with a big prize flower with toxic petals and a polluted earth.

The organic approach is to get out of the competition; plant the flower; give it natural fertilizer, sunlight, and water; see how big it grows, and assume that's as big as it's meant to be. There's no prize and no comparing. Just lots of flowers of many sizes and colors.

Similarly, the organic way to form relationships is to be honest and accept that we can't force a special bond to develop. A special partner or kindred spirit is a gift from the Universe. So instead of thinking, "Now I've got to do this right so he or she will like me," try thinking, "I will be myself and see what happens. I will trust my inner sense of timing and see if there's a fit. If I stay true to myself then the rest is out of my hands."

An organic concept of health would be to use natural remedies for healing whenever possible—human connections, herbs, exercise, meditation, lowering stress, expressing feelings, natural foods, relaxation, and joy. Going deeper, we would focus on preventing disease by living in a healthy, balanced way, nurturing the intertwined nature of mind, body, and spirit.

One amazing example of an organic approach to a medical problem is that poor mothers in a South American country, who had premature births and no access to medical care, made a sling to carry their babies over their left breast and heart on a twenty-four-hour basis. They were called "Kangaroo babies" and did extraordinarily well. Yet in our country it was considered a radical step in need of expensive research to let parents of premature babies have a few minutes to take these children out of incubators and hold them. And hospitals have made up fancy words for touch, such as *tactile stimulation*. When we think in an organic way, simply letting our experience guide us, we know in all our being that touch, caring words, and kindness are healing.

Organic also means trusting that deep within us we have a Knowing place, a source of wisdom and truth that is our guide and our spiritual center. One of my attractions to Quaker meetings for worship is that we all sit in a circle and if people feel called to speak about something of a spiritual nature they do, and if no one does we sit in silence. That way the gatherings are alive, ever-changing, and emanate solely from the inner world of those who attend. This can be a model for human relationships—simple, clear, emanating from our heartfelt truths and surrounded by moments of stillness and just being.

94. STOP CHASING AFTER GOLD, THERE'S ONLY A POT OF BAKED BEANS AT THE END OF THE RAINBOW

We search, we struggle, we strive, we adventure. We cross the river and seek our heart's desire. But like Dorothy in *The Wizard of Oz*, there's a part of us that simply wants to come home—home to ourselves, to simplicity. There was a cartoon in the *New Yorker* portraying a man running toward the end of the rainbow only to see a pot of

baked beans there. Whenever I think of striving for something I think of that image and realize it's time to stop, breathe, and remember there's beauty in the ordinary and it's right here.

Recently I visited a dear old friend whom I hadn't seen for nearly twenty years. He greeted me warmly and introduced me to his dog. His sense of graciousness and ritual was as I remembered. His house was orderly and simple. I had mentioned that I wanted only fruit and tea for breakfast, and I arrived to a neatly set table with an orange and apple on a plate beside a knife, a mug, and a newspaper on the same green tablecloth I had sat at twenty-five years before. I also saw the same bookshelves, the same tables, the same dishes, and the same couch as before. In a passing moment, a painful image flashed through my mind of the thousands of dollars I had spent on such items over the years and how little they mattered. How peaceful it was to be with him in this uncluttered home. I hold that image in my mind as I struggle to detach from wanting more things.

I went through a period of buying lots of pretty things in a compulsive way. I would buy something, and then after I had enjoyed it for a little while, I would start thinking about the next thing I would buy. One day a catalogue came in the mail with pictures of beautiful quilt covers, and I started to fill out the order form. Then a part of me said, "No, stop." And as if I were led, I walked upstairs to my bedroom and sat down on my plain, natural cotton comforter and rubbed my hand over it. I said to myself, "Isn't this beautiful. It's mine, it's paid for, and it's restful. It is enough." Again and again I need to quell my restless mind and remind myself, *This is enough.* What I really seek is more love, more peace, and more free time.

So next time you sit down to a simple supper, crawl into a cozy bed, have a warm chat with a friend—imagine that you *are* at the end of the rainbow. This is it. This is life, and it's wonderful just in this moment.

95. EXPRESS GRATITUDE

Expressing gratitude ignites the light within us and is a sure path to joy. Gratitude is one of the highest vibrations of energy we can create, it's free, and anyone can give it. It can be as simple as being thankful for soup, being thankful one can see, walk, wiggle a finger, or tap to a beat. One can be grateful for healthy children, good neighbors, good luck, and simply being alive.

It's been two and a half years since I had cancer surgery, and I seldom think about it anymore because it appears to have been caught early. Yet I recently felt compelled to attend a benefit for cancer survivors. It was an outside affair at a high school with music, food, and various events. At the beginning, everyone who had survived cancer or were struggling with it walked together around a field track. We were young and old and in between. Walking with that group of people, I felt overwhelmed with a sense of gratitude for being alive. There was so much joy on the faces of the people walking, many whose days are in short supply. I flashed on all the memories of the shock, the fear, the worry, and the friends who supported me, and I could feel the gratitude living in me.

Sometimes we forget to be grateful until we survive a trauma. For example, after having the flu when you ache all over, throw up for hours, and have little people pounding in your head with hammers, it is sheer bliss just to eat a piece of toast, walk outside without getting dizzy, and breathe fresh air. *Part of the journey toward joy involves not waiting around for trouble, but being continuously aware of our blessings.*

A very intimate way to connect with another person is through a sense of shared gratitude and awe. When I lived in Minneapolis, my friend Adair and I walked around Lake Harriet through all the seasons. Sometimes we hardly talked except to say, "Oh look at how the ripples in the water go in different directions." "See the purple and green design on the sail of that wind-surfing boat." "Oh, look, the Canadian geese have returned." Sometimes we would sit and watch the sun reflecting on the water or the sky turning coral while the moon rose on the other side of the lake. I struggle to find words to express the feeling. It was like being enveloped together in a cocoon of happiness, made more intense by my friend's quiet presence.

Tuning into gratitude is like hearing a song reverberating within. It is in many ways the soul finding its voice. And when that voice speaks of happiness and joy, the energy is infectious, bringing hope and spirit to others.

96. WALK THROUGH FEAR, AGAIN AND AGAIN

Walking through fears and limitations is a big part of the journey to joy. A life moving toward joy will be a dance between relaxing in your comfort zone, and stretching your limits, be they physical, psychological, or spiritual. There are the big leaps we take—leaving jobs or relationships, finding a new home, starting a new relationship, going scuba diving—but more often there are small steps that need to be taken over and over again, frequently in the face of discomfort and fear.

As a psychologist, I have heard many people justify not stepping forward in their lives by saying, "But I'm afraid." My answer is, "Fear is no excuse for not doing something." Either we move forward or we don't. It's important to recognize our fear. It can take on many forms—forgetting, boredom, irritation, hostility, disdain, sleepiness, running away, or getting scattered. Learn to recognize your particular symptoms of fear so you can say, "Oh. That's just my fear. I can do it anyway."

If you wait for fear to go away before you take action, you may never start. Pushing through fear can include telling someone you love them, telling someone you are upset, buying yourself flowers, talking about sexuality, renewing an old friendship, sitting quietly in a chair for ten minutes, climbing a mountain, not eating sugar, going to a movie alone, or telling someone, "I'm afraid," "I'm lonely," or, "I'm proud of myself." I remember the terror when I first started expressing any form of anger. I was sure I would be abandoned. Although a few people left me, others became closer friends and my body and mind became more relaxed.

One way to help nudge yourself through fear is to ask, *What do I have to gain?* You might make a new friend. You might have fun, might learn something, might get a better job. You might have a new experience, come closer to your heart. And while it's possible you might regret it, remember all decisions are made with insufficient data. When we think of all the things we have to gain from expanding the boundaries of our lives, we help counteract the automatic, "But what if . . . " side that dances to the tune of fear. Remember, it's better to ask for what you want and hear a no than to sit on the sidelines of life. Amid the noes you'll get a few yeses as well.

Moving through fear, like many of the steps toward joy, takes practice and discipline. The more we make little changes on a daily basis, the more we are prepared for big changes. Over time we learn that we won't fall apart in the face of change, we can tolerate the unknown, even find it exciting and full of joy.

97. FREE YOUR SPIRIT

When a group of students were anxiously asking their spiritual teacher questions about God, he replied, "God is the Unknown and the Unknowable. Every statement about God, every answer to your questions is a distortion of the truth."

The response was shocking to the students. "Then why do you spend so much time speaking about God?" they asked.

"Why does the bird sing?" was the sage's reply.

Recently I went on a camping trip and it rained, snowed, was hot and sunny, and I felt at times energetic, tired, happy, lonely, peaceful, and connected. When I can embrace all of these moments as part of a whole, none better or worse than the others, then I am feeling close to the spirit or God/Goddess that is a mosaic of all that is.

In our search to find Joy there is ultimately no way to put words to the experience, yet, if we think about it, most of us are seeking joy. Sometimes the journey appears more like an avoidance of pain, yet even then we are trying to feel better. If the spirit is one with our inner Knowing place, then to find joy we free the spirit to merge with the magical world we live in.

More deeply, we free our spirit when we feel love for ourselves and others. As life goes on we learn that the joy is in the loving. We love others and give to them because it feels good to us. Our blessings become richer as we share them with others. Ultimately, loving and being loved feel inseparable because we see all people as living within the same circle. We have a consciousness of "us" rather then "me versus you."

Ken Keyes writes about using the phrase "one of us . . . " whenever we get into thoughts that separate us from others. "One of us is upset." "One of us is angry." "One of us is being generous and kind." Said repeatedly, this phrase has a profound ability to shift our perceptions of oneself as separate from others.

Once we have experienced the dwelling place of the spirit—of joy and love and an "us" mentality—the more that troubles and frustrations pass before us like in a movie rather than swallowing up our lives. We may get mired, confused, tired, or lonely sometimes, but like homing pigeons, we keep heading back to joy, that safe haven for our spirit and our soul.

98. LET THE DANCE DANCE YOU

As I finish this book, I sit here looking through my file folder of thoughts and ideas on joy, thinking, "Oh, dear, I've forgotten to talk about singing as part of joy, and I don't think I included the quote on not waiting for holy days, rather to make all days holy, and . . . " Then I laugh. *Of course I haven't said everything.* We *never* remember all our thoughts or follow a course just as we had planned. And that's what happens when we let the dance dance us.

When we dance with life we become co-creators of that mysterious sense of energy that comes through us saying, "Yes, do this," or "No, don't bother with that." The result may not be what we had planned, but if it comes from following the rhythm of the beat, and going where we are led, then it is the best we can do. For a moment we may feel sadness about the path we didn't follow or the words we didn't say—but our power lies in returning to the belief that we did the best we could at any given moment, and this is the way it is. We are standing in the center of life, being as honest as we can be. We may do it differently next time, but we can never take away the past. We can laugh at it, or cry over it, but eventually, if we want to return to joy, we will come back to the present and go on from here.

99. DANCE AND SING AND MAKE MERRY IN THE MOONLIGHT, SUNLIGHT, RAIN, OR SNOW

Many people resist "growing up" because their image of an adult is a serious, weary, boring person who works too hard and seldom has fun. I suggest we absorb the image of playfulness and spontaneity into our image of adulthood so that playfulness and joy are highly valued. On the path toward joy, the idea is to increase our ability on a daily basis to let loose, be spontaneous, and send our observing critic to the winds. For many people this involves a process of releasing repressed memories and feelings.

Sometime between my childhood and my thirties, my ability to play and be spontaneous slowly faded into a debilitating depression. At age thirty, when I started my journey back to life, I went to a disco with a group of friends. When they moved out to dance, I just stood there, frozen. Where was that child who could run, play, leap, and dance? I felt so sad and wondered if I'd ever feel free again.

Last winter—at age fifty-four— under a brilliant full moon, I went with a few dear friends out in the deep snow in a large open field near my house to play. We jumped up and down and huddled together making our shadows dance in the moonlight. Then we started running in expanding concentric circles, howling like coyotes. At first I was self-conscious, aware of being in the snow with friends, but at some point, as we started running in circles and howling, the mantle of self-consciousness slipped away. The howl from my belly resonated within me like a cello string and I felt a primitive connection to earth, moon, animals, and snow. And in that moment I was free, one with magic.

It feels as if a thousand years of therapy, workshops, and prayer intervened between the time I stood like a statue watching my friends dance and the few precious moments of surrender to joy in the snow.

The journey to joy takes time. It is a process of awakening and of letting go of the rules and "shoulds" and beliefs that strangle our passions and creativity. Yet every moment when we are at peace—at one with our lives, the earth, and our loved ones—is worth a million precious gems. It is truly the richness our spirit seeks.

JOY TO THE WORLD

100. BLESS THE PLANET WITH YOUR JOY

When you radiate happiness, you become a touchstone for others, providing inspiration and hope. Your energy contributes to bringing peace and harmony to other people and to the planet. If we love life and love our neighbors, then we will love and care for the source of life, the earth.

In case you need a rationalization to reach for joy, remember, in a world full of joy it is inconceivable that we would plow under grain fields while people starve. It is inconceivable that we would have homeless people or children dying without medical care amid millionaires, or that incest and abuse would be tolerated. In a world that values joy and love, all forms of war, violence, and killing would be considered archaic because we would start learning from an early age how to share, talk, and compromise. We would approach decision making with the philosophy that our personal joy is connected to all people being cared for. If joy for all meant that many of us would need to live with fewer material possessions, it would not feel like a sacrifice but rather as part of the give and take of love.

We are given a life—a precious commodity—and are placed on this earth for a short while. We are surrounded by incredible beauty, strength, and love along with incredible violence, hatred, and prejudice. Every time a person becomes happier, they are moving one step away from prejudice and violence and closer to love and compassion.

So think of your personal joy as a contribution to peace on the planet as well as food for your spirit. Filling yourself with joy takes you into a world with the "peace that passeth understanding."

101. REMEMBER, ALL LOVE IS GOD'S LOVE

We have a great deal of division in this world that dictates who you are allowed to love at a personal, intimate level. Black–white, Protestant–Catholic, Muslim–Hindu, Jewish–Palestinian are a few of the many divisions people are taught not to cross. And if you are lesbian or gay you're told to forget intimate love altogether.

Fortunately, people's deeper level of spirituality allows them to fall in love and in doing so break down these barriers. Imagine a world where we blessed all love as God's love no matter what our faith, race, ethnic background, color, or sexual preference. Recently I read of a young woman and man from warring factions in Yugoslavia who were shot as they attempted to run away together. Recently, another article showed a gray-haired man in a military dress uniform with numerous medals embracing a male partner wearing a banner that read, "I got medals for killing men and a discharge for loving one."

Because love and joy are so totally intertwined, bringing joy to the planet means supporting all love between all people on the planet. Part of the consciousness of joy is realizing we are all more alike than different. The desire to belong, be respected, live free of fear, work with dignity and purpose, and find joy are common to all people. Of course we have different customs, histories, and traditions, but when we reach deep enough, we will find the commonalities and in doing so find joy.

I remember a workshop at the International Decade of Women's Conference in Nairobi, Kenya, 1985, where a Palestinian woman and an Israeli woman struggled to talk about their political differences. The interchange was heated, painful, difficult, and heartfelt. It was also riveting to listen to. As I partook of this event I felt as if I was somehow at the center of the universe and it was cracking open to something better, and as I had that image something cracked open in me and I felt the tears come to my eyes.

Every time we cross a barrier, we build a bridge. And as we build bridges on the outside, we heal the division within us. As a result, we all have more territory to walk on, and more people to love, and more peace on the planet.

Author's Surprise

You start at the beginning, go on until you get to the end, then stop.

Lewis Carroll

Well, here I am. Two entries didn't get into the final table of contents, so I am confronted with the task of either going back and cutting something out, which I really don't want to do, or letting the book write me, which I have decided to do. So, you may feel let down because you were ready to be done by 101, or you may tell yourself you are getting more than you paid for. Two more.

102. LOVE THE LAND THAT LOVES YOU BACK

We need to make peace with the fact that we are all completely, utterly, and unquestionably dependent on the earth for the food, air, and water that sustains our lives. Because the earth is the source of life, it has been referred to as Mother Earth or Gaia.

Peter Russell, referring to Dr. James Lovelock, a British chemist and inventor, writes in *The Global Brain,* "The entire range of living matter on Earth, from viruses to whales, from algae to oaks, plus the air, the oceans and the land surface all appear to be part of a giant system able to regulate the temperature and the composition of the air, sea, and soil so as to ensure the survival of life."

To live at one with the spirit of life we need to relinquish the patriarchal image of man having dominion over the earth, and accept that we are an *integral* part of life on earth, neither higher nor lower than any other part even though we have the ability to think.

The concept of ecology refers to an understanding of the interwoven nature of all life. To date, we have had artificial polarities among people wanting to protect wildlife, people wanting to build dams to create electricity, and people wanting to protect jobs. Everyone gets in their corner and argues for their turf. We need to reach a point where we see all the problems and all the solutions as interdependent. Again, we need an "us" mentality.

Here is an example that illustrates the compartmentalized decision making that has gone on for the past decades: I went canoeing on the Flathead River in Montana with a group of friends. There was no way to gauge the speed of the river because it changes dramatically hour by hour because of the hydroelectric dam upstream—it changes the flow to coincide with electrical needs. In addition to being dangerous to inexperienced canoers, the sudden changes in flow are highly destructive to the fish population.

I believe there is a way for people to have electricity, for the fish to live in the river, and for the river to flow at a reasonable speed without sudden dangerous shifts so families with young children can be safe canoeing.

We get stuck seeking solutions because we approach them

with a negative mind-set, fear letting go of old ways, resist stretching our comfort level, or don't have the skills to do consensus problem solving. *We need to believe it's possible to live in peace with people, animals, and the earth, bring this consciousness to all decision-making processes, and work together to find solutions that affirm all life.*

Humankind is at a crossroads in it relationship to the earth. As Russell says, in the course of evolution, humankind may turn out to have been a cancer that visited the earth for a while, "consuming in decades resources that Gaia herself inherited billions of years ago, and threatening the biological fabric that took millennia to create." He also suggests that if we stop our predatory behavior, we could live on the earth operating more as a global brain. As a crucial part of our journey to joy, we need to use our wisdom and creativity for helping humankind become a "global brain" rather than an instrument of devastation of the earth. We also need to realize that humankind has become an endangered species.

We have talked about joy as coming from small steps we take on a daily basis. Easing the burden on the planet will start from the daily practice of millions of people taking a few small steps. Imagine if one million people drank one less can of soda a week—that would be fifty-two million fewer cans for the world to cope with a year. Every time you use less, recycle, buy unpackaged foods, use natural substances, and avoid herbicides, you become part of the global brain.

The important thing to realize is that *everything you do to help, matters.* And just as giving love to others increases our joy, so does caring for the earth help us live in peace with ourselves, because we are living more in harmony with the source of our life.

103. LIVE IN COMMUNITY WITH ALL

A healthy community is central to joy. Community is a place to call home, a safe haven where people reach out their arms, draw you in, comfort you, cheer for your awakening power, and cherish you just the way you are—fears, tears, humor, and all. Community is a group of people committed to individuals and to the whole, a place where your voice is heard and valued, a place where you can drop the mask.

People have a natural need to attach and bond with others. Without a healthy community to embrace us, we fill in the empty places with dependent relationships, hoping they will provide the security we long for. But no one person can provide an island of safety for any of us, and there is no all-wise person who can give us the answers. When we lack community, our longing for connection gets turned into a longing for chocolate, sugar, sex, caffeine, drugs, work—something to fill up a nameless restless-

ness that churns away inside. But a cookie can never replace a hug. We need to realize that we are tribal people, meant to live together, and that our joy comes when we work side by side, laughing together, learning from each other, savoring the journey.

Our concept of community expands as we grow. When we are very young, it includes our family and then includes our neighbors, our religious institutions, our schools, our workplace, and the town we live in. For many, it stops there. But on the path toward joy there is a constant expansion of community until it includes all the people on the planet, as well as the planet itself. We internalize the awareness that we come from one and the same Creator—we live on one earth, in one ecosystem, with one people, who are on one journey.

Schiller, in his "Ode to Joy," wrote, "Millions in our arms we gather, to the world our kiss be sent." Imagine a love inside of you so expansive that you feel an invincible cord of light connecting you to all people. Imagine diverse groups of people all over the world gathering in small groups to take turns telling the story of their lives to each other. Imagine, as we listen to each other, the walls of separateness melting away and our hearts opening to each other. Imagine knowing that you are not alone with your hopes, dreams, fears, and joys. So reach out, listen, learn, be gentle with yourself. Remember that ultimately your personal joy is tied to the joy of all people and all life on the earth.

Peace and joy in abundance to you and your loved ones . . . and to all people.

HOW TO CONTACT
THE AUTHOR AND ILLUSTRATOR

Charlotte Kasl
Many Roads, One Journey
P.O. Box 1302
Lolo, MT 59847

Charlotte Kasl presents workshops and talks on sexuality, addiction, healing, spirituality, empowerment, and joy based on *Women, Sex, and Addiction: A Search for Love and Power; Many Roads, One Journey: Moving Beyond the 12 Steps;* and *Finding Joy: 101 Ways to Free Your Spirit and Dance with Life.* She also does organizational consulting to resolve conflict and help people work together with greater understanding and efficiency. For workshop information, please enclose a legal-size self-addressed, stamped envelope.

Please note: Although I love to hear from people and read every letter, I cannot always respond personally, and I don't have references for therapists around the country.

Lenore Davis, Illustrator and Soft Sculptor
Box 47
Newport, KY 41072